Schematic Adaptation of Brian Cambourne's Model of Learning

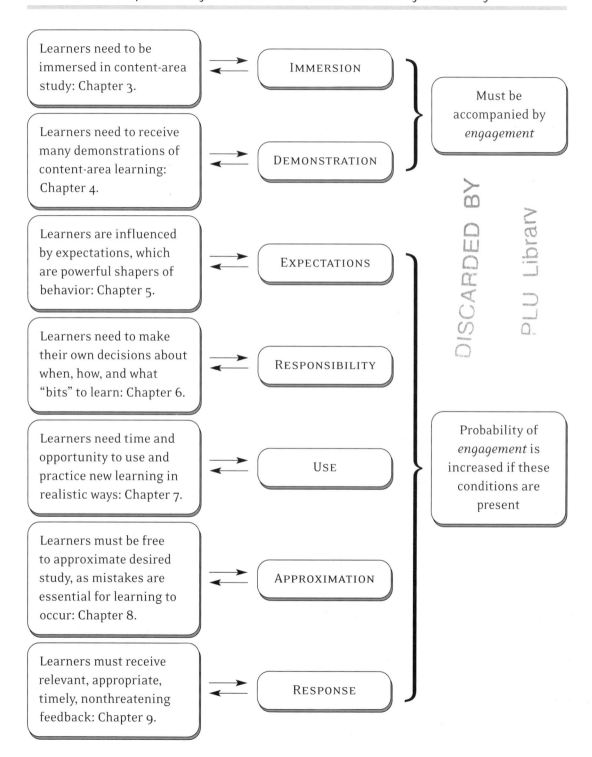

Learners need to be immersed in content-area study: Chapter 3.

IMMERSION

Learners need to receive many demonstrations of content-area learning: Chapter 4.

DEMONSTRATION

Must be accompanied by *engagement*

Learners are influenced by expectations, which are powerful shapers of behavior: Chapter 5.

EXPECTATIONS

Learners need to make their own decisions about when, how, and what "bits" to learn: Chapter 6.

RESPONSIBILITY

Learners need time and opportunity to use and practice new learning in realistic ways: Chapter 7.

USE

Probability of *engagement* is increased if these conditions are present

Learners must be free to approximate desired study, as mistakes are essential for learning to occur: Chapter 8.

APPROXIMATION

Learners must receive relevant, appropriate, timely, nonthreatening feedback: Chapter 9.

RESPONSE

Engaging Adolescent Learners

A Guide for Content-Area Teachers

RELEAH COSSETT LENT

Foreword by Brian Cambourne

HEINEMANN *∬* PORTSMOUTH, NH

HEINEMANN
A division of Reed Elsevier Inc.
361 Hanover Street
Portsmouth, NH 03801-3912
www.heinemann.com

Offices and agents throughout the world

Library of Congress Cataloging-in-Publication Data
Lent, ReLeah Cossett.
   Engaging adolescent learners : a guide for content-area teachers / ReLeah Cossett Lent.
       p. cm.
   Includes bibliographical references and index.
   ISBN 0-325-00843-4 (alk. paper)
   1. Active learning. 2. Effective teaching. 3. Thought and thinking—Study and teaching (Secondary). I. Title.
LB1027.23.L46 2006
373.1102—dc22   2005025913

Acquisitions Editor: Lois Bridges
Editor: Gloria Pipkin
Production: Lynne Costa
Cover design: Catherine Hawkes, Cat & Mouse
Typesetter: Eric Rosenbloom
Manufacturing: Steve Bernier

Printed in the United States of America on acid-free paper
10   09   08   07   06   VP   1   2   3   4   5

To my husband,
BERT,
the most engaging person
I have ever known

Contents

Foreword

Brian Cambourne

At the end of the recent academic year, I asked my students to evaluate the preservice teacher education program they had just completed. When asked to comment on the value (if any) of the theoretical components of the course, one thoughtful student's response captured the essence of the majority of opinions:

> We learn all about these theories of children's physical, cognitive, social, emotional, and linguistic growth. We study these things from Piaget's, Vygotsky's, Gardner's, Chomsky's, and other theorists' perspectives. But when a group of twenty-five or thirty individual children turn up on day one of the school year and are put into your class, their learning behavior can be explained by neither the sum total nor different bits of all these theorists' theories. We still don't have a valid theory that can explain how to orchestrate the overwhelming complexity of the typical classroom. (B. Teach. graduate 2004)

If I've learned one thing from forty years' engagement in teacher education, it's that classroom practitioners are not typically enamored with theory. They become particularly irritated when competing theories add to their confusion. They are disappointed by the lack of real-world relevance of these theories; the lack of congruence between research-based knowledge and the messy complexity of the real world is a perennial problem. Schon informs us that teachers are caught between the "high, hard hill of research-based knowledge" that overlooks the "soft, slimy, swamp of real life" (Schon 1987). Those who look to the theories "up on the hill" typically find they are of little use in addressing the complex problems "down in the swamp."

Early in my academic career, in order to avoid being similarly perceived by the teachers with whom I worked, I asked them to extend me the privilege of trying out my ideas in their classrooms. When I managed to get myself into a pedagogical mess, often they would rescue me. Once they did this, I knew I had coresearchers who would help me turn any vague theoretical ideas I might develop into workable classroom practice. The learning theory known as Cambourne's Conditions of Learning was developed this way, in the swamp as it were, with the help of a range of brilliant classroom practitioners such as Jan Turbill, Andrea Butler, Hazel Brown, Di Martin, and many others, all of whom showed me how theory could be turned into practice.

What does all this have to do with ReLeah Lent's book? Simply this: The way she's turned my theoretical ideas into classroom practice in United States high schools puts her in the same category as those brilliant classroom practitioners mentioned above. Through her book, Lent becomes my de facto coresearcher who shows me once again "how theory can be turned into (classroom) practice," this time in ways that *engage adolescent learners.*

In this book, Lent takes my theoretical ideas on a practical classroom journey through the complex world of high school classrooms and adolescent learning. This is a journey I'd never contemplated, mainly because adolescents and their confusing hormonal behaviour scared me. With Lent's book in my briefcase, however, my apprehension toward venturing into middle and high school classrooms is diminishing. She not only interprets my ideas accurately, she also extends them in ways that make sense. High school teachers who've often wondered how to engage adolescents more deeply in reading, writing, and other accoutrements of effective literacy learning will find the strategies and lessons described in *Engaging Adolescent Learners* extremely helpful in draining their own particular classroom swamps. As we are wont to say in Australia, "This book is a bloody good read, mate!"

Acknowledgments

I began teaching in my early twenties, and it was as a teacher that I first became a real student. My first teaching position at Mowat Middle School was a transformational experience that laid the foundation for my later practices and beliefs. There I met Gloria Pipkin, a gifted teacher who was to become a lifelong friend, coauthor, and now my editor. Our relationship has sustained and inspired me throughout the years. Other colleagues in that famed English department, specifically Terry Rubin and Nancy Goodwin, have remained personal and professional muses during my educational journey. Ben Dykema, my team teacher and close friend, taught me about myself as an individual and as a learner, helping me find magic in the classroom. The years we spent as colearners with our students were unparalled. But the greatest gratitude goes to my students, many thousands of them, who contributed their gifts to this book.

In 2000, I left the classroom to take a position as a literacy coordinator with the Florida Literacy and Reading Excellence Project (FLaRE) housed at the University of Central Florida, and it was here that the second stage of my schooling began.

Pat Striplin, the first director, took me to new heights by allowing me to discover my strengths in an environment where I was free to take intellectual risks. She taught me to fill my own well before attempting to fill others and helped me turn my love for books into a vehicle for motivating teachers. It was at FLaRE that I formed relationships with committed professionals who would influence my thinking and help me transfer my experiences into knowledge: Susan Kelly, my brilliant friend who continually pushed me to "go deeper"; April Johnson, always there to support me when I fell; Connie Cain and Marcia Halpin, who gave me insights into myself as a teacher and learner; Enrique Puig, who loaned me his signed copy of Cambourne's *The Whole Story* when I began writing this book; and Larry Bedenbaugh, who patiently answered my questions concerning the role of technology in learning. My FLaRE assistant and dear friend, Lyn Leeuw, was with me every step of the way, providing encouragement, laughter, and the most wonderful cherry cheesecake in the world.

I must also acknowledge the professionals at Heinemann, the best in the business: Lois Bridges for her unwavering support of my sometimes unconventional ideas; Maura Sullivan for her guidance with the cover; Lynne Costa, my wonderful production editor; Steve Bernier, manufacturing; and Amy Rowe, editorial assistant.

And then there is my family, my constant and loving supporters. My husband, Bert, knows this book as well as I do and has contributed his own considerable talents to its making. My father, too, read every word on these pages, providing keen and loving insights.

So, it is with deep appreciation and gratitude that I acknowledge family, colleagues, and friends who make up my own learning community, one whose collective voice is reflected throughout the pages of this book.

Introduction

If [the teacher] is indeed wise he does not bid
you enter the house of his wisdom, but rather
leads you to the threshold of your own mind.

—KAHLIL GIBRAN

The very culture of secondary education is changing day by day. Teachers are reporting that many students are not coming to school, and when they do, they are passive, often disengaged and disinterested; or worst, literally asleep. They may respond when asked a direct question, but their thoughts are far away from the four walls of most U.S. classrooms. Even so-called advanced students frequently are not motivated to learn anything more than is necessary to obtain a passing grade. In fact, it has become a badge of honor for many students to figure out how to appear to be working while actually doing little or nothing. Cheating is rampant and after-school jobs consume more and more of teenagers' energy and passion. The concept of learning as an inherently joyful act is overshadowed by gaining credits, passing tests, and advancing through the ranks until graduation. A recent survey from Indiana University reported that fewer than half of the student respondents said their schoolwork makes them curious to learn about other things and fewer than one third said they were excited about their classes (Tebbs and Shaughnessy 2005).

This discouraging downward trend has not gone unnoticed by politicians and educational gurus who insist that no child will be left behind if the bar is raised by retaining students or not permitting them to graduate until they have demonstrated learning gains on a standardized test. Paradoxically, the proffered solution, like many quick fixes to complex challenges, is a gloss job of legislative mandates that whitewashes the fence without noticing the rotting boards underneath. Mandating learning will not increase students' ability to learn or teachers' ability to teach. It will provide a percentile score for measurement, a standardized box into which students may fall, but it will not touch the heart of learning.

This spiraling logic leaves teachers dizzy and breathless. Although strong in their content areas, many secondary teachers have now come to believe they have been missing the mark all of these years—that new "scientifically-based reading" is a subject unto itself, one that transcends traditional subject matter. With increasing requirements by state and federal governments, content-area teachers are under pressure to enroll in on-line or state-endorsed reading courses in order to be certified as "highly qualified," but this massive training has too often turned teachers into frenetic strategy users without understanding how or when to employ strategies appropriately. States such as Florida have even adopted a formula for teaching reading: $5 + 3 + ii + iii$. Teachers are instructed to take the five elements of reading (phonics, phonemic awareness, vocabulary, fluency, and comprehension), add three types of assessment (screening, diagnostic, and progress monitoring), provide initial instruction, and, for those students who aren't reading on grade level, initiate immediate intensive intervention. It is interesting to note what is missing from the formula: motivation, readiness, interest, background experiences, text, context, and the reader. Glib sound bites that contort the complex process of reading and learning into contrived formulas and packaged programs tied neatly in a bundle rarely work for real teachers facing hundreds of students who are anything but formulaic. Students, confounded with monitoring their own fluency rates, interacting with computer programs armed with artificial intelligence, and rereading passages of isolated text, are like young Houdinis, trying to untangle the ropes to set their learning free. In the meantime, subjects that engage and motivate students—such as music, art, ROTC, and vocational topics—are being eliminated to make way for test-prep classses. Field trips and extracurricular activities that support content-area studies and make learning meaningful are eliminated or postponed until after the all-important testing date. Engagement seems to have little, if any, role in learning.

When common sense gives way to narrow research and testing hysteria, when schools all over the county ignore the developmental needs and interests of the learner, as well as the expertise of the teacher, an educational revolution is inevitable. If teachers must produce statistics that can be scored, standardized, and filed in cumulative folders to keep their jobs, they will invariably resort to canned learning materials and practice test samples. Students will continue to respond negatively to such pressure, becoming anxious, fearful, and oppositional—or simply give up in anticipation of what may happen to them if they don't perform. The thrill of discovery, the certainty of students' own abilities, the very essence of learning is in danger of suffocating under an avalanche of multiple-choice questions.

Is it possible to satisfy the testocrats and, at the same time, infuse students with a quickening for learning? Can we slow the hands of bureaucratic time so that we can meet the needs of students where they are, not where we expect them to fall on a continuum? By coming to understand the complex facets of learning, the importance of engagement, and the power of learning communities, it *is* possible for teachers to transform their own instructional practices within the confines of educational mandates. A shift in thinking about what it means to learn and a measure of trust in both teachers and students will achieve what all the mandates in the world cannot. It is possible for secondary classes to be intensely academic and also to deeply engage adolescent learners. Students can score well on standardized tests as a natural by-product of meaningful learning, and teachers can freely engage in curriculum topics beyond the confines of the test. By adhering to basic learning principles, school can be a place where thoughtful writing, wide reading, and lifelong critical thinking will become a mainstay of education in the United States.

Section One

The Nature of Engagement

The whole art of teaching is only the art of
awakening the natural curiosity of young minds
for the purpose of satisfying it afterwards.

—ANATOLE FRANCE

Learning is infused with engagement. The act of taking in knowledge and transforming it so that it becomes a part of oneself, much like the act of taking in food for sustenance, is undeniably, inherently engaging. Without the cerebral act of learning or the physical act of eating, our species would cease to exist. The idea of forcing this process on unwilling adolescents or coercing learning by threatening punishment is a paradoxical and rather barbaric concept. Perhaps our most important task is to help students discover and use their intrinsic desire for engagement as a means of tapping into learning that will sustain them in the future.

Section I examines a theoretical framework, Brian Cambourne's conditions for learning, that defines such engagement and offers a variety of classroom practices and study group activities intended to turn the concept of engagement into a lifelong avocation.

1

Learning Through Engagement

Knowledge of methods alone will not suffice;
there must be the desire, the will to employ them.

—JOHN DEWEY

Thinking About Learning

Perhaps the best place to begin is to ask questions we may not be able to answer fully, questions that deserve much consideration and discussion: *What does it mean to learn? What is engagement?*

We know that that one of the most effective ways to learn is through engagement, and a primary factor in engagement is a connection to one's own experience, background, and interests. Using that premise as a jumping-off point, take time to reflect on your learning and teaching. Discuss the following questions in a group or with a coteacher as a way to internalize the process of learning.

◆ Think back to a time when you had to learn something very difficult, perhaps for a course or your job, such as a new computer program. What type of pressure were you under to learn? Were you successful? What was the most difficult part of the learning? The easiest?

◆ Think about to a time when you enjoyed learning something. What made the learning rewarding? Has your learning about that topic continued? Do you think you had a natural affinity for the learning?

◆ Think about a teacher or mentor who helped you learn something. Did the teacher directly instruct you? Provide feedback? Facilitate your own learning?

◆ How would you define learning? Is it a process? Are there different types of learning?

◆ What factors engage you in learning?

◆ Does your own teaching style reflect your definition of learning?

◆ Think back to a student who told you that he or she truly learned something in your class. What prompted the comment?

◆ Think about a time when it was difficult to help your students learn. What were the circumstances?

◆ Think about close friends, your own children, or siblings. Review their triumphant and traumatic learning experiences. What made them so?

As you may have discovered while answering the questions, learning is rarely linear. Despite the mandate that schools must make adequate yearly progress, we all realize that the most effective learning occurs when we make mistakes or digress, often in a circular, not a linear, fashion. Probing, thinking through and beyond the problem, revising courses of action, making connections, and using past experiences are authentic ways that humans progress and learn. It is the process of learning, not the progress in learning, that defines thought.

Many teachers confuse standards or curriculum with learning. These tools may help teachers and administrators manage the business of education, but deep learning is rarely standardized. Consider the idea of curriculum as a suggested menu of the vast amount of knowledge, facts, and skills accessible to students in their learning quest. Think of textbooks as rich resources that organize knowledge in an easily accessible form, not as an infallible guide for all subjects. Imagine *using* standards for guidance, much as new parents use childcare books to gain information about general stages of child development and not regarding those standards as sacred proclamations. Suppose we view learning as the ability to think, reason, and explore what one needs to know when one needs to know it. What would schools look like if all classrooms were bastions of thought where "habits of mind" were sharpened, much as Project 2060: Science for All Americans (Ritchhart 2002) proposed with these questions:

Evidence: How do we know?

Viewpoint: Who is speaking?

Connections: What causes this?

Supposition: How might things be different?

Meaningfulness: What's the point? Why does it matter?

If such questions were an intrinsic part of learning for every subject area, imagine the depth of understanding that students would acquire. They would practice *how* to learn, not *what* to learn.

For example, think of one topic or unit of study that is a part of your curriculum. Use the above questions to set the purpose for a lesson within the unit. Below is an example of how such questions could be used as an exploration of the Civil War.

Learning About the Civil War

Evidence

◆ Are the resources I am giving my students true and accurate?

◆ What primary-based documents or other materials could help supply evidence of events during the Civil War?

Viewpoint

◆ Whose viewpoint will students hear when they study this unit?

◆ How many viewpoints could be examined in studying the Civil War?

Connections

◆ What were the causes of the Civil War?

◆ How can those causes be linked to current events, personal experiences, or students' background knowledge?

Suppositions

◆ How could things have been different?

◆ Will we repeat the past?

Meaningfulness

◆ Why does it matter that we study the Civil War?

◆ In the grand scheme of U.S. history, what role did the Civil War play?

Engaged Learning

The concept of engagement is not easy to bullet and categorize—it is both individualized and fleeting, a combination difficult to capture. John Guthrie and Emily Anderson, who have spent years studying engagement, point out that a "self-determining learner" is one who possesses intrinsic motivation that creates energy (Guthrie and Alvermann 1999). They see engagement as a dynamic system directly related to motivation. Martha McCarthy, director of the High School Survey of Student Engagement, points out that engagement is multifaceted: "In addition to the important behavioral component, it has an emotional aspect and a cognitive component. Engaged students get more from school on all levels than do their disengaged peers" (Tebbs and Shaughnessy 2005, 2). John Dewey coined the term *reflective inquiry*, which explains engagement as a process of identifying problems, studying them through active engagement and then reaching a conclusion or solving a problem.

Although engagement is necessary for learning, it is infinitely easier to define than to create. There is no one product or practice with a guarantee for engagement; the notion is simply too complex and ever-changing. The best we, as teachers, can do is be aware of its importance and seek it at every turn.

For example, consider how you might engage students in learning about the Civil War by asking them what would make the study engaging for them. Before beginning the study about the Civil War, have students brainstorm questions that will make the topic engaging and meaningful to them. Their questions might include:

- Is it necessary to memorize the dates or names of battles to learn about the Civil War? How do such facts help me understand the Civil War?

- Could we read historical fiction, such as *Cold Mountain*, and gain an accurate understanding of the Civil War?

- How helpful are internet sites in knowing about the Civil War?

- Could we watch videos of the Civil War in addition to reading about it?

- Could we choose topics that interest us, work in groups, and share with the entire class in place of reading from the textbook?

- What if we learned about the Civil War last year (or the year before)? Why do we have to study the same topic again this year?

If engagement is at the center of learning, then students are at the center of engagement. Without acknowledging that truism, it is impossible to consider the topic in a meaningful way. Research on learning consistently refers to affective factors—motivation, goals, environment, interest—and yet often the content is placed at the top of our to-do lists without remembering that content by itself is powerless. Knowledge, information, and facts lose all efficacy without human beings who have the desire, as well as the ability, to transform them into instruments that will do their bidding. Frequently, knowledge is forgotten when the bell rings to end the period because the affective dimension of learning has not been tapped by the teacher. This important piece begins with knowing students and helping them come to know themselves.

Affective and Emotional Learning: Brain Research

> We now recognize that our brain isn't limited by considerations that are applicable to machines. Thoughts, feelings, and actions, rather than mechanical laws, determine the health of our brain.
>
> —RICHARD RESTAK, *THE NEW BRAIN*

Although we have learned more about how the brain functions during the past three years than we have in the last decade, much of this research has been used to promote political agendas, specifically regarding young readers—and too often the important emotional activation is ignored as if it were not a part of valid research. According to neural scientist Joseph LeDoux, who has studied the brain connections of emotion, cognition, and memory, "These interconnections mean that emotions and cognition are integrated and interactive and that an emotional response can, in terms of pathway activity, precede a cognitive perception and response" (Coles 2004). It should come as no surprise, then, that teachers who appeal to their students on a personal, emotional level are ones that open the floodgates to forceful learning.

Fortunately, good teachers don't need scans of their students' brains to know how to help them learn. They have long realized that students must make connections to what they already know; students must have a contextually organized framework for new learning, and they must come to see the learning as their own. The danger in relying too heavily on the latest brain research is that we may forget our own instincts as teachers. As Parker Palmer points out, aesthetically rather than scientifically, in his book *The Courage to Teach* (1998), "Good teachers join self and subject and students in the fabric of life." If American's educational fabric is fraying, it may be because of current trends that narrow learning to discrete bits of information rather than weaving the teacher, the subject, and the student into threads of discourse, knowledge, and relevance that create a strong and beautiful fabric.

Who Are You? Survey for Students

Encourage students to supplement their survey (perhaps on poster board or in a folder) with magazine pictures, drawings, poetry, essays, or photographs. Allow students to share their answers in a group or with the entire class if they feel comfortable doing so as a way to begin building community.

1. Estimate the amount of time you spend each day:
    - watching TV
    - playing video games
    - using the computer
    - reading
    - spending time with friends
    - being outside
    - playing sports
    - doing homework
    - spending time with family
    - working at an outside job
    - other: _____

2. Describe how you would spend a perfect day.
    - What would you do?
    - Where would you go?
    - Who would you spend time with?

3. What do you like best about school? Least?

4. If you could create a brand new school, what five things would you include in your plans for the school?

5. What is something you've done in your life that makes you proud?

6. What do you want to learn in this class?

7. Who is the most important person in your life? Why?

8. What qualities do you value most in friends?

9. How do others describe you?

10. Who are you?

FIGURE 1.1

Although it is still considered scientifically unsophisticated in some circles to admit the significance of the *affective* aspect of learning, any enlightened teacher will attest to its merit. Students who are hungry, tired, or anxious have more difficulty learning than those who are well-fed, rested, and secure. Sensory stimuli, such as movement, laughter, art, and music, produce measurable effects on learners' brains as well as on their motivation for learning. A safe environment where students feel free to make mistakes while learning, or at the very least are encouraged to take intellectual risks, is also a factor often ignored when dealing only with the quantitative results of learning. The irrefutable fact is that each student is a collage of varying interests, natural inclinations, inherent modalities, and distinctive personalities. Add environmental and genetic backgrounds to this mix, and the statistical probability that any one student is even similar to another, much less standardized, is highly unlikely.

We must first know our students before we can hope to help them learn. Most teachers have some type of get-acquainted activity at the beginning of the course, such as the survey in Figure 1.1. This should be only a first step, however, in a daily interaction that leads to an increased understanding of students' academic and personal talents, challenges, and characteristics. It is important to send a clear message that the human aspect of our students is more important than their test scores.

Learning as Understanding

Education is not the filling of a pail, but the lighting of a fire.

—WILLIAM BUTLER YEATS

Today's students need to know more than the ubiquitous information on the World Wide Web. They must know how to transform that information into *understanding* as a way of creating their own fabric of life. How can brain research and the affective realm of learning become fused into understanding? James Zull, in *The Art of Changing the Brain* (2002), makes three points in explaining what happens to the brain when information is changed into understanding. First, he contends, the brain must *transform* from past to future:

> Our experience is the past, by definition, but the ideas we create are for actions we will do in the future. They are plans. Without this transformation we rely totally on the past and our reflections about it. Ultimately, we rely on memory. But if we use our experience to

produce new thoughts and actions, we create a future. The potential of knowledge gained in this way is unlimited, and it can change how and what we do indefinitely into the future. (33)

Second, Zull sees the brain as turning the outside experience into internal knowledge and understanding. This process that comes from within as the brain creates new knowledge is what he calls *taking ownership of learning:*

> It is a change in the learner from a receiver to a producer. Since we do not rely on the outside for understanding, we do not have to wait for new information to arrive to deepen our comprehension. We can move from passive to active and become creators of knowledge. (33)

The third aspect is the transformation of power. We know what we need for further learning and will take charge of getting it rather than remaining dependent on others. It is this third step that Zull refers to as *deep learning.*

The current focus on standardized testing, state standards, and a pre-set curriculum often makes learning dependent on others—specifically on teachers or textbooks—and doesn't allow students to become creators of knowledge. Weeks, sometimes months, of valuable learning time are spent having students plod mindlessly through practice test items and testing protocols. The process of deep learning, of owning knowledge and conceptually processing it, takes time and flexibility. Similarly, strategies, the new silver bullets of learning, often impede this vital process. Whole faculties sometimes march lockstep through books of strategies, using one per week in every class, not understanding that strategies are to be used as instructional tools, not as replacements for worksheets. If strategies could be worn as good undergarments—unseen support to enhance the outer appearance and make the wearer feel secure—they would be far more effective. Too many teachers see strategies as the clothes themselves and feel students are fully dressed once they have mastered the strategy. Good strategies, like good underwear, must take into account the different sizes and shapes of the wearer. Not all strategies work for all students, and they must learn how and when to rely on strategies to help them learn. While most strategy teaching is certainly an improvement over students sitting in rows listening to lectures, we must use strategies as vehicles to move students from receivers of knowledge to producers of it. Using strategies wisely requires understanding and appropriately recognizing today's students as those who have been born into a world that is vastly different from the one that welcomed students even a few years ago.

It is a beneficial exercise for teams, departments, or study groups to discuss their students' collective characteristics in an effort to become conscious of how they change from year to year. Such awareness will help teachers see their students for who they are, not replicas of other students who have occupied the same seats in years past. Below is an exercise that will help teachers look at students realistically.

Students: Then and Now

Choose a typical student from your first year of teaching. How would you describe that student regarding:

- attention span
- motivation
- background knowledge
- attitude toward learning
- aptitude toward content
- technology interests and skills
- intellectual strengths and challenges
- physical appearance

Now, think of a typical student from this year.

- How is this year's student similar or different from the one you described above?
- What trends have you noticed in students since you first started teaching?
- How do you describe this student when you discuss him with other teachers, parents, or guidance counselors?
- How have your teaching practices changed to meet the needs of today's students?

Learning for the Future

Our job, as educators, is to prepare our students for their futures. This job today is especially challenging, because, for the first time in history, we cannot clearly describe the future for which we are preparing our children. Our world and the information that describes it are changing too quickly. The very nature of information is changing: how you find it, what it looks like, the way it behaves, where it comes from.

—DAVID WARLICK, *REDEFINING LITERACY FOR THE 21ST CENTURY*

Because we have at our keyboarded fingertips more information than we ever dreamed possible about learning, it is difficult to stay on top of the latest research. The information age continues to both overwhelm and enlighten us. Just as teachers are inundated with information in every form—professional books, articles, conferences, videos, internet sites—information overload is a serious threat to students, especially information that is not relevant to their lives and appears to have little purpose other than for passing a test. Such an overload can cause their brains to shut down, and students retreat inwardly as a way of coping. Often this inward action manifests itself in outward behaviors, such as apathy, acting out, or defiance—putting the skids on engagement.

Despite teachers' best intentions to satisfy both their students' inherent interest in learning and the federal edicts that demand students know unrelated items of information for testing purposes, there are many factors over which teachers have no control. Students come to school from places far removed from the secondary classroom environment. In *The New Brain,* Richard Restak reports that the modern world has literally changed the functioning of the brains of our students due to the abundance of stimulation and increasing amounts of information. "The brain," Restak says, "has had to make fundamental adjustments. Thanks to technology, each of us exists simultaneously in not just one *here* but in several" (2003, 52). Students can watch TV about events halfway across the globe while at the same time monitoring a split screen with a movie about man-eating dinosaurs. They can email friends in another city, talk on the cell phone to a parent, and watch a sports event in Miami at the same time. It is not uncommon for a teenager to sit in front of a computer with three or more open windows, simultaneously engaged in instant messaging, visiting in a chat room, and playing a digital game. Students feel secure within the complexities of their own personal computers, much like children snuggled with stuffed animals in days past. This digital generation is infinitely more complex than any generation preceding it, and with information doubling every one to three years, there is little slowdown in sight. Students live in a virtual womb of technology.

In addition, as Restak points out, "our brain is being forced to manage increasing amounts of information within shorter and shorter time intervals" (48). Everything is instant: microwaved dinners, whirling motion on cable music channels, rapid-fire video games, online ordering of goods and services. Multitasking is the modus operandi of our society, even for very young children, as they flip through television channels while eating cereal and slipping on their velcroed tennis shoes. Increased noise, speed, and activity have changed students from tortoises to hares, rarely stopping to rest for fear of being left behind. In the midst of this physical and mental cacophony, students enter another type of virtual world: the classroom. They must then adjust their controls to slow motion as they pass from the rooms of their daily lives to an unfamiliar place, a land where bells denote segments of activity, silence is rewarded, and a single test predicts their futures.

Compounding the problems in this unnatural environment is the fact that an estimated 17 million people in the United States have been diagnosed with attention deficit disorder (Amen 2001), many of them children and teens. Autism, once a relatively rare disorder, is now described as epidemic. It is naive to think that the classroom as we know it today will meet the specialized needs of all of our students for a future we can hardly imagine.

As if all of that weren't enough to make teachers want to walk out of the door and never return—as many do in increasing numbers—they must now take into account the individual characteristics of each student's learning profile, such as Howard Gardner's work on multiple intelligences or Daniel Goleman's insights on emotional intelligence. Learning is not one-dimensional, as we once believed. (See Chapter 12 for additional information on these topics).

These theories have added substance to the current buzz notion of differentiating instruction to meet the needs of all learners, but many secondary teachers are unable to fathom, much less implement, differentiation in a classroom with increasing numbers of students and the associated data collection. Add this to the logjam of mandates and requirements based on the No Child Left Behind legislation, and the profession of teaching begins to look more like a clinical laboratory than a place where human beings discover the wonders of life.

Schools of the future must be prepared to embrace the complexity of the individual by facilitating, supporting, and empowering learners. We must trust our own intuitions and encourage students to do the same. Learning is not a commodity that belongs to a few stakeholders. It is a part of what makes us all connected, despite political, religious, or social differences—a global inalienable right. It is our obligation to protect that right for our students.

Learning with Cambourne

Powerful, critical, active, productive literacy can be achieved systematically, regularly and relatively painlessly, with larger numbers of the school population, if certain learning principles are understood and practiced.

—BRIAN CAMBOURNE

Understanding Learning

We do not understand what we do not possess.

—GOETHE

How is it possible for today's teachers to address the complex factors that have molded students into such unique individuals? How can each student's learning needs be met with the incredible demands placed upon teachers by district, state, and federal mandates? Utilizing one particular program or textbook—no matter how much we have spent on it—or adhering to a preset curriculum often only skims the surface of learning and leaves both students and teachers frustrated. It is clear to many educators in the trenches that the current demands and challenges are driving an ailing system to its knees.

With the unrelenting push for every student to achieve a basic level of literacy for the purpose of graduating in order to become a productive worker, we have left behind one of the most valuable goals of education: to provide the student with an active, ongoing system for learning and enjoying the intellectual complexities of life. By shifting our pedagogical constructs, perhaps by changing the very language we use to describe the act of *schooling*, we can create classrooms where learning is meaningful, relevant, authentic, *and* rigorous. Once we, as educators, establish a theoretical framework for learning, we can help students maximize their brains' incredible potential to learn, store, retrieve, and apply information.

Consider, then, an alternative approach to learning, one that starts with a strong theoretical foundation that supports the infinite number of factors involved in learning. Such a framework would act as a buffer between outside demands and classroom instructional practices. It would encourage each student to find deep meaning in all areas of the curriculum and facilitate learning as a lifelong process. It would be overarching and well-researched, yet accessible. It would be adaptable and non-subject specific. It would come without political strings or corporate ties; its profit would be counted by students' increased interest in learning and teachers' increased interest in teaching. It would be a framework that applies to all learning inside and outside of school.

Such a framework *does* exist; it is called Cambourne's conditions of learning. A representation of Brian Cambourne's model of learning can be found in Figure 2.1. What rings true about this model is that engagement is the bull's eye—the very core of learning. Transforming information to understanding requires engagement on the part of the learner. Without engagement, learning becomes a series of dance steps that never find the rhythm.

Brian Cambourne, head of the Centre for Studies in Literacy at Wollongong University in Australia, has researched the conditions of learning for more than twenty years. His theories have been used successfully by thousands of teachers in schools in Australia, New Zealand, the United States, and Canada. Each of the conditions illustrated in Figure 2.1 is briefly reviewed below, as described by Cambourne (1995). Section II of this book provides specific examples of how the conditions of learning can be applied to content-area classes, along with suggestions for engaging students in learning.

Cambourne's Conditions of Learning

◆ *Immersion* Learners are "saturated by, enveloped in, flooded by, steeped in, or constantly bathed in that which is to be learned" (185). They must be immersed in all types of experiences that allow them opportunities for reading, writing, speaking, and listening.

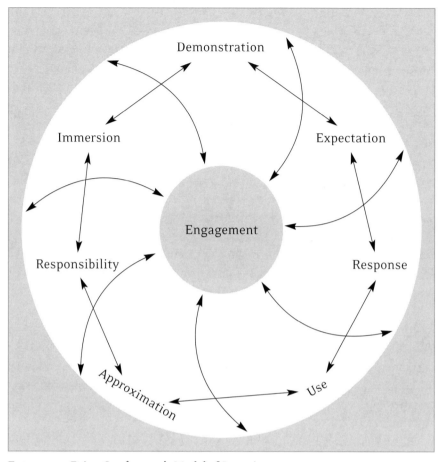

FIGURE 2.1 *Brian Cambourne's Model of Learning*

- ◆ *Demonstration* Learners "observe (see, hear, witness, experience, feel, study, explore) actions and artifacts." They must have many demonstrations and models of desired behaviors that allow opportunities for students to observe and later attempt learning.

- ◆ *Expectations* Learners receive messages from the one who is providing the learning experience. Expectations are "subtle and powerful coercers of behavior." The learner must hold expectations for himself that he can and will succeed, but teachers must also hold high, realistic expectations for the learner.

- ◆ *Responsibility* Learners are "permitted to make some decisions (i.e., take responsibility) about what they'll engage with and what they'll ignore." Factors such as when, what, and how regarding the learning are a part of the decision-making process. The teacher must show the leaner how to acquire and maintain responsibility.

- *Approximations* Learners approximate learning or, as Cambourne says, "have a go at it." They are not expected to have mastered the learning, and there should be no anxiety associated with the experimentation. Learners must feel safe to take risks and make mistakes. They need to know that their attempts at learning are vital and important steps in the process. Mistakes are essential for learning to occur.

- *Use* Learners must have ample opportunities for using and practicing the new learning. They must learn how to apply concepts and take control over learning. This must take place in relevant settings while doing authentic tasks.

- *Response* Learners must have appropriate feedback from knowledgeable others. Responses should be "relevant, appropriate, timely, readily available, and nonthreatening, with no strings attached" (1995, 187).

Cambourne describes engagement as the result of having the above conditions in place. The qualities inherent in such engagement include giving attention to the learning, perceiving a need or purpose for the learning, active participation in the learning, and, often, participating in risk taking. When analyzing your own learning, you will probably recognize that engagement, however you wish to define it, is an essential quality for deep learning. If you have ever sat through a driving class to keep points off your license, you will recognize the difference between motivation to complete a task or receive a passing grade and intrinsic engagement in learning.

Demonstrating Learning

We teach people how to remember, we never teach them how to grow.

—Oscar Wilde

Cambourne's principles of engagement further help us understand how demonstration of the learning, or modeling, is a fundamental prerequisite for engagement to occur. Research confirms the importance of demonstrating learning, and most elementary teachers understand that scaffolding, or the gradual release of responsibility to the student, is a natural process that leads to independent learning.

Demonstrating learning has three steps: *I will show you how to do it, we will do it together,* and *you will do it alone.* Secondary students often find themselves facing just the last step with instructions such as write an essay, work this problem, read this text, or create a project. Teachers frequently believe that students have had sufficient demonstration in previous grades and omit this important process.

Not surprisingly, learners are more likely to engage deeply with demonstrations if they believe that they are capable of ultimately doing whatever is being demonstrated. Furthermore, they must believe that the demonstration has some potential value, purpose, and use for them, in an atmosphere free from anxiety. Most of us can verify that premise by thinking of our own learning, but the importance of those beliefs somehow becomes lost in the formalized school setting. Paying attention to the learner's affective needs and providing a realistic purpose for learning in a safe environment are basic and important components if we want the learning to stick. In addition, it is vital that the person who demonstrates the learning is someone whom the learner likes, respects, admires, trusts, and would like to emulate. Relationships matter a great deal.

Cambourne's model of learning is often used to show how learning applies to literacy and is extremely familiar to many elementary teachers who focus on the process of reading. Its implications for secondary content areas, however, are immense, especially considering the current emphasis on reading in middle and high schools. In fact, it is possible that the application of Cambourne's conditions of learning could transform secondary education as we know it today—classrooms could become places where learning, not testing, is the order of the day. Once we change our perspective of the "school" and imagine it as a place where students come together to use their brains in ways they were designed to be used, the contagious synergy will be much like an athletic team coming together to use their bodies as they have been designed. Learning will no longer be defined only by grades or test scores; it will become the natural product of the brain's potential—a tangible force spreading from student to student, teacher to teacher, school to school. It *is* possible to ignite the embers of a long-dormant educational system by building a sustainable fire from within rather than mandating quick flashes that are destined to burn out.

3

Immersion in Learning

I read most of my book last night. I have never read that much in one night. Most of the time I read for maybe 10–15 minutes but never for a couple of hours. I lost track of time, I never looked up at the clock. I really started to get to the point where I thought that I was a person in the story, just there watching and listening. If I could read like that every time, I could finish my book in two days.

—TENTH-GRADE STUDENT'S JOURNAL
RESPONSE TO *OF MICE AND MEN*

Immersion Through Experience

Think about a hobby or class in which you became completely immersed, where time ceased to exist, where you lost awareness of yourself as you focused exclusively on what you were reading, thinking, learning, or doing. Try to identify the characteristics of your immersion:

◆ Where were you?

◆ How much time did you spend in the immersion?

◆ Was the task or learning difficult?

◆ Was testing or evaluation a part of the experience?

◆ What was your motivation for engaging in the experience?

◆ Was the learning valuable to you? If so, in what way?

As Brian Cambourne (1995) suggests, immersion is a critical aspect of all learning. Just as the avid fishing enthusiast spends hours at the tackle shop checking out the latest equipment and every free moment trolling the waters, most engaged learners are immersed in their chosen subject. Childcare classes in high school tapped into this concept long ago when students carried computerized babies that cried, wet, and had to be fed on demand, even in the middle of the night. If you want students to understand what it's like to have a baby, then immerse them in childcare. Thus it is with learners in a classroom. If we want students to learn to read, they must be immersed in text. If we want them to become scholars of world history, they must be surrounded with biographies, documents, maps, historical texts, pictures, and all types of primary sources. Imagine learning to use a computer with only a textbook that describes its functions or learning to play a musical instrument with only a how-to guide. Without immersion, the subject becomes a dry treatise, something that is viewed from the outside instead of experienced from within. Students can learn about a topic short-term for the purpose of passing a test or reciting facts, but those who internalize concepts and catch the fire of learning are those who cocreate with the subject.

One of the easiest ways to ignite students' passions is by creating a setting of immersion: a classroom overflowing with interesting supplemental texts, objects, and resources. Young adult literature and nonfiction texts that tap a variety of interests are as close as the nearest bookstore or catalog, usually with hefty educator discounts. Related magazine articles are also compelling to learners because of the visual aspect of the presentation. Photographs, graphics, and short articles that can be read in one sitting give students a chance to view the world through another medium. Current newspapers and magazines will eventually pull in reluctant readers as more motivated students share and discuss their discoveries.

With the current push for literacy of all kinds, grants to purchase reading materials are also readily available, with titles to supplement every subject area. But having books in the classroom isn't enough; immersion means more than availability. It means that the atmosphere, the very culture of the classroom is such that students can't help becoming engaged. It is similar to entering an electronics store where televisions surround the customer, where reality is altered with the voices and images of people who exist on another level. The immersion, while virtual, is nonetheless real at the moment, and one cannot help but be drawn into the other world. Following are some ways in which teachers and students can work together to create a classroom library rich with immersion materials.

◆ Students can sponsor a community magazine drive. Local professionals may donate specialty magazines that deal with subjects such as psychology, health, science, and engineering.

◆ Students can donate books or magazines from home to the class library once they have finished reading them and no longer want them. Create bookplates from sticky labels that acknowledge the donors.

◆ Make a deal with business partners: In exchange for grants to supply a classroom library, students can write reviews of the newly donated books in a monthly newsletter that includes a page thanking sponsors. Students could also "sell" space for business cards or small advertisements in their newsletters—much as school newspapers, yearbook staffs, or sports programs do—to generate funds for books.

◆ Partner with a local bookstore to supply new books in exchange for student reviews that can be displayed in the store. Consider approaching local nonprofit organizations for similar partnerships.

◆ Offer to review books for major young adult book publishers in exchange for copies of newly published books.

◆ Students can organize a student reading team and sponsor monthly book fairs by partnering with a local bookstore. Bookstores generally donate 20 percent of the profit to the school.

◆ Keep your class library current and relevant to students by making book catalogs available to students so they can choose books that interest them. Provide booklists and reviews of young adult literature through the following sources:

   ◆ American Library Association (www.ala.org)

   ◆ The ALAN Review (a publication of reviews and articles regarding young adult literature from the National Council of Teachers of English)

   ◆ Richie's Picks online service (http://richiespicks.com)

   ◆ www.teenreads.com

Elementary teachers understand the importance of displaying student work, but in secondary classes the walls are often bare, as if an environment free of distraction will somehow create more intellectual thought. A key component of engagement is placing students in an environment that speaks of their success. What better way to immerse students in content than to provide examples of learning by using walls to frame students' writing, drawings, photographs, or projects? Some examples include:

◆ Students in a marine biology class became immersed in the subject by turning their classroom into a marine biology art studio. They painted a mural on the wall with anatomically correct sea creatures. Together, students researched marine life, blocked the scene, experimented with paint that captured the colors of the ocean, and spent hours after class working on the project. The class was physically and intellectually immersed in marine biology.

◆ Students in an English class worked in pairs to photograph representations of lines from poetry and displayed the photos alongside poster-sized copies of the poems, eventually donating them to an elementary school media center where younger students were introduced to poetry through the photographs.

◆ Students in a high school U.S. government class used *Time* magazines for years to supplement the curriculum, and each week's cover was taped on the wall beside the previous week's cover to form a *Time*line. Students had a visual reminder of what they had been reading, and the living history wall continued to teach them.

◆ As students in a reading class discussed Lois Lowry's *Gathering Blue*, the teacher recorded on a chart memorable lines from the discussion. Students' names were placed under their chosen quotes and the poster remained on the wall for the rest of the semester. At the end of the course, a student asked to take the chart home and hang it on her own bedroom wall as a reminder of the class.

Photography, journalism, drama, band, and art classes are good examples of immersion in secondary schools. These subjects are usually popular with students and the experiences they have in such classes stay with them for a lifetime, often leading to careers as journalists, photographers, or actors. While the nature of so-called elective curriculum may be inherently more engaging to students than traditional academic subjects, immersion in content-area studies goes a long way toward creating similar motivations that transfer to real-life options.

Anticipation Questions

Anticipation or prediction guides are used in many classes as a way of engaging students in text prior to beginning a unit of study, but in some classes they are little more than worksheets that students fill out without giving the statements much thought. ROTC instructor John Gross, head of his school's reading team, changed the concept of anticipation guides to anticipation *questions* that get students right into the middle of the action. He used the following questions to generate discussions, hypothesis, and heated debate among his high school students before a study of the Normandy Invasion. Notice how the questions contain words that spark interest and create a genuine sense of curiosity.

1. What was the theme song of the invasion?

2. Why did the Americans and British repaint every aircraft in their inventories right before the invasion?

3. What role did rubber dummies play in the invasion?

4. Why did U.S. soldiers borrow fire ladders from the London fire department?

5. What Walt Disney character played a role in the invasion?

6. What were Rhinos and Mulberries?

7. Who led the attack with a musical instrument?

8. What part did animals play in the battle?

9. Children's toys were used by twenty thousand soldiers. What were the toys and how were they used?

10. Why was the weatherman more important than General Eisenhower?

Immersion Through Others

> The best educated human being is the one who understands most about the life in which he is placed.
>
> —HELEN KELLER

Today's students—who cut their teeth on technology—often long for interaction with a real human being. Former students who have become successful in a given field, instructors from the local college, and professionals from the community can guide students into a three-dimensional world, showing them the relevance of learning as they answer questions and personally interact with students. Often parents have a talent or specialized knowledge they will share if provided the opportunity—and if the class culture is one that encourages learning outside the confines of the textbook. Conferences and symposiums intended for teachers or professionals may welcome student participation or even create a special session for students if arrangements are made in advance. Businesses and local government officials will also make space for students when they have special speakers, events, or community forums.

As a journalism teacher, I was once invited to be on the advisory board of a local television station. I asked if one of my students could join the board; the station manager said he hadn't thought of including a student, but promptly agreed. This student provided valuable insights and thoughtful comments that helped guide the station's decisions throughout the year.

Students are often excluded from other valuable learning opportunities commonly afforded to teachers, such as hearing authors speak at state and national literacy conferences. Recently, Sharon Draper, author of many popular young adult novels, was a speaker at a reading conference I attended. I wondered how many students would have loved to hear her talk about her books, many of which are ones that first introduced them to the magic of reading. Several years ago when my students were reading Robert Cormier's novel *I Am the Cheese,* AT&T donated the equipment for a class conference call with Cormier. I set an appointed time for my students to talk with him, and it was as if he were there with us. Students became engaged in a discussion with the author that was far deeper than any I may have facilitated.

Immersion Through Writing

The pen is the tongue of the mind.

—MIGUEL DE CERVANTES

Writing is often overlooked as a valuable means of immersion because of the mistaken concept that reading is somehow separate and apart from writing. As reciprocal processes—one reads writing; one writes reading—students need to be shown that relationship in everything they do. Writing is a powerful way of understanding and internalizing information for many students, and they should be provided the opportunity to write each day. Five-minute quickwrites, with prompts such as "How do you think the term *values* in an algebraic equation came to have its name?" give students an alternate venue for thinking about the topic. Having students use a learning log to record thoughts and questions also helps make writing a natural part of any subject. Once students see that writing can be a tool for their own learning and they become comfortable with the mechanics of writing, they may incorporate the practice of writing into their own learning repertoire. Such "writing as a way of knowing" should not be graded beyond a completion mark, of course, but the cumulative value of having students process their thinking through writing will yield long-term gains that, inevitably, will show up in graded assignments. Following are some ways to immerse students in writing.

◆ Put blank poster board or chart paper on the wall with a question that requires thought, perhaps related to a current event, such as "If cars become a luxury item only for those who can afford exorbitant gas prices, what will your life be like as an adult?" Encourage students to respond both to the question and to each other's comments before, during, and after class. Encourage students to create weekly prompts.

◆ Begin the class each day by providing students with a prompt or question related to the previous day's discussion or reading. Have students write quietly for five minutes. Some students have never processed their thinking by writing; once they become accustomed to this practice, it may become a lifelong learning tool.

◆ Put pertinent quotes on the board or assign students as quote finders, and have students respond to the quotes as a way to end class. Many students collect quotes from lyrics, books, television shows, or movies, and such quotes can be catalysts for stretching their thinking and making valuable connections to other learning.

◆ Create a journal or learning log for each student that stays in a box or file drawer in the classroom. Have students staple notebook paper inside a plain manila file folder and personalize the front with quotes, drawings, or pictures. Students should have free access to their own folders and decide for themselves when to use them. Ask them to respond to or question anything in class they don't understand. At the students' discretion, they may ask the teacher to read and reply to their questions. This process allows shy or reluctant students a venue for deeper understanding.

◆ Have students create class booklets or newsletters related to topics studied in class. Students are often eager to take on the roles of editor, writer, researcher, typist, or artist. An added advantage is the community that emerges as students work together on enriching their learning through a common product.

◆ Form writer's circles where students write in response to learning and have on-paper discussions, similar to online chats.

Immersion Through Interactive Displays and Books

It is the imagination that gives shape to the universe.

—Barry Lopez

Secondary school media centers often have beautiful displays of thematic books or books related to holidays, but do these displays immerse students in learning or simply provide a school backdrop? How many students, for example, rush by the Holocaust-themed books arranged tastefully around *The Diary of Anne Frank* or quickly glance at a Black History Month exhibit constructed because it happens to be that time of year? Notice how carefully students read every word on a homemade campaign sign for a class officer taped to the wall, yet they ignore expensive showcases full of colorful, slick learning aids.

By thinking of engagement as the core of all the conditions for learning, common practices begin to take on different perspectives. Can students become immersed in a subject without being fully engaged? Can students become fully engaged without taking responsibility for the immersion? If students provided the artifacts for the immersion, would they pay more attention? Think of a topic that you teach each year. Brainstorm how you and your students could create a classroom that immerses them in the subject. Below is an example of immersion in a geography class about to embark upon a study of Pakistan. Student teams are responsible for different aspects of the country and expand the topic by creating pertinent interest centers.

Immersion in Study of Pakistan

◆ Create a display of young adult literature from the media center related to Pakistan, such as *Shabanu: Daughter of the Wind* (Staples).

◆ Download maps of Pakistan from internet sites and hang them on classroom walls.

◆ Provide past issues of newsmagazine articles chronicling current events in Pakistan.

- Play Pakistani music as students enter the class.

- Show clips of movies set in or near Pakistan to help students visualize the country.

- Provide folders containing pictures and information of animals, plants, and weather patterns in Pakistan.

- Find a guest speaker from Pakistan to answer students' questions.

Below is an example of an interdisciplinary unit on literature and historical events related to the Russian Revolution.

Immersion in Literature/History of the Russian Revolution

- Read the novel *Animal Farm* (Orwell) in English class.

- Examine the historical role of each animal's counterpart in the Russian Revolution in history class.

- Provide copies of young adult novels and nonfiction related to the topic for small group reading or content-area learning circles. Titles include:

  - *The Quest for Anastasia: Solving the Mystery of the Lost Romanovs* (Massie)

  - *Anastasia: The Last Duchess* (Meyer)

  - *The Last Tsar: The Life and Death of Nicholas II* (Radzinsky)

  - *The Fate of the Romanovs* (King)

  - *The Russian Revolution (Living Through History Series)* (Campling)

- Have students research related topics and create interest centers for the classroom, media center, or hall bulletin boards, including:

  - prominent figures from the time: Rasputin, Anastasia, Nicholas, Alexandra, Lenin, Trotsky

  - a comparison of the lifestyle of the aristocracy and the proletariat: diet, clothing, dwellings, work environment, leisure time activities

  - a history of the Russian ballet

  - Russian authors who lived during the time period, such as Leo Tolstoy (introduce Tolstoy through *The Three Questions* [Muth], based on a story by Tolstoy)

- Show the classic film *Nicholas and Alexandra* as an after-school event or in cooperation with a local movie theater.

Francis Bacon said, "Some books are to be tasted, others to be swallowed and some are to be chewed and digested." Often in secondary classes we insist that students digest every book on the syllabus, especially if it is appealing to our own palate. There are many books that students might want to simply taste or chew on for a while. Comic books, graphic novels, art books, or nonfiction informational books, such as *Life* magazine's *Our Century in Pictures for Young People,* Scholastic's *Voices from the Fields: Children of Migrant Farm Workers Tell Their Stories,* or even Uncle John's Bathroom Reader series by John Scalzi are instantly engaging to most students.

Don't dismiss picture books as being only for children; renowned writers and artists are now adding their talents to this genre and are creating books with sophisticated text, beautiful art, and provocative themes. Using picture books in secondary classrooms to engage students and introduce topics is an enjoyable way to hook them. These books are also perfect for reluctant or struggling readers who can appreciate them without feeling that they are being placed in a "low-level" reader.

Picture Books for Content-Area Studies

Art

Michelangelo by Diane Stanley

Over the Rainbow by E. Y. Harburg; paintings by Maxfield Parrish

Seurat and La Grande Jatte by Robert Burleigh

English/Language Arts

The Big Box by Toni Morrison

The Man Who Walked Between the Towers by Mordicai Gerstein

To Hell with Dying by Alice Walker

The Three Questions, Based on a Story by Leo Tolstoy by Jon Muth

A Midsummer Night's Dream retold by Bruce Coville

Shakespeare and Macbeth: The Story Behind the Play by Stewart Ross

Squids Will be Squids: Fresh Morals, Beastly Fables by Jon Scieszka and Lane Smith

William Shakespeare and the Globe by Aliki

Multicultural Literature

The Day Gogo Went to Vote by E. Batezat Sisulu (African)

Grandfather's Journey by Allen Say (bridging of U.S. and Japanese cultures)

The Lotus Seed by Sherry Garland (Vietnam)

Mufaro's Beautiful Daughters: An African Tale by John Steptoe

The Secret Footprints by Julia Alvarez (Dominican Republic)

Math

The Grapes of Math by Greg Tang

Math Appeal by Greg Tang

Sir Cumference and the Dragon of Pi: A Math Adventure by Cindy Neuschwander

Music

A Band of Angels: A Story Inspired by the Jubilee Singers by Deborah Hopkinson

Blues Journey by Walter Dean Myers (written as a blues song)

Duke Ellington by Andrea Davis Pinkney

When Maria Sang by Pam Munoz Ryan (biography of Marian Anderson)

Poetry

At Break of Day by Nikki Grimes

Freedom Like Sunlight: Praise Songs for Black Americans by J. Patrick Lewis

Harlem by Walter Dean Myers

Life Doesn't Frighten Me by Maya Angelou

Poetry for Young People Series: *Robert Frost*

Wonderful Words: Poems About Reading, Writing, Speaking, and Listening selected by Lee Bennett Hopkins

Science

Everglades by Jean Craighead George

The Great Kapok Tree: A Tale of the Amazon Rain Forest by Lynne Cherry

Insect-Lo-Pedia: Young Naturalists Handbook by Matthew Reinhart

Spiders Spin Webs by Yvonne Winer

Starry Messenger: Galileo Galilei by Peter Sis

Social Studies

Dear Benjamin Banneker by Andrea Davis Pinkney

The Greek News: Alexander Victorious! by Anton Powell and Philip Steele

Malcolm X: A Fire Burning Brightly by Walter Dean Myers

Music For Alice by Allen Say

Smoky Night by Eve Bunting

Rose Blanche by Roberto Innocenti

Spirit of Endurance: The True Story of the Shackleton Expedition to the Antarctic by Jennifer Armstrong

The Yellow Star: The Legend of King Christian X of Denmark by Carmen Agra Deedy

Under the Quilt of Night by Deborah Hopkinson

The Wall by Eve Bunting

Immersion in learning doesn't require that the teacher spend night and day creating an engaging classroom culture. In fact, the more immersion work the students take on, the greater the learning. Not all students will be interested in every topic, of course, but creating the expectation for extended learning and fostering a climate of immersion will enhance all lessons, as well as providing students the opportunity to utilize their various learning styles. In a climate of immersion, students discover that learning is as natural as paying attention to what is all around them.

Immersion Tip for Second Language Learners

Immersion can take on new meaning for second language learners. Just as these students learn the customs, social norms, and culture of their new home, they also learn from other students if they are immersed in the subject from various perspectives. Motivation is essential for these learners, and being a part of a classroom where the playing field is leveled through a variety of learning activities and artifacts will provide the necessary confidence for students who are struggling to learn a second language. The goal to create a climate where all learners have equal opportunities to explore and grow through a variety of experiences is one that is attainable by all teachers for all students.

Immersion: Study Groups for Teachers

The benefits of teacher study groups are innumerable. They create synergy, cohesion, and commitment as well as increasing teacher knowledge and refining skills. Studies have shown that students in schools where teachers participate in study groups achieve at higher levels than in schools where there are no study groups. In addition, teachers in schools that implement study groups report an increased efficacy and enjoyment with their jobs.

Just as immersion is a condition for learning with students, it is also one for teachers. Although it may seem that there is not an extra minute in the day, finding time for participation in study groups is an important and satisfying experience. The next several chapters target specific topics for group study, but following are the basic steps in starting a study group.

Teacher Study Group: Planning

1. What are we hoping to achieve through our study?
2. How will the group be organized (by teams, departments, interest, need)? Number of members? Role of members?
3. What are the logistics of the meeting: time, place, length?
4. How will our group's study positively affect student learning?
5. How will we deal with challenges, such finding time for meeting and sustaining momentum?
6. Who will be the facilitator? Will the role remain with this person or rotate through the members?
7. Who will keep notes? How will they be kept? Who will have access to the notes?
8. How will the group ensure reflection time?
9. What resource(s) are needed for study?
10. How will we share what we've learned with students, other faculty members, the district, or a wider audience?

Teacher Study Group: Reflection

A major part of the work of a teacher study group is reflection. This can be done through writing, dialogue, brainstorming, or simply quiet thinking time. Without time to reflect, the knowledge teachers gain from the study may lie dormant and unused. Reflection questions can include:

◆ Why is this issue one that matters to me as a teacher?

◆ How will this study affect my students' learning?

◆ What issues related to this topic have created a challenge for my students or me in the past?

◆ What have I learned that will affect my teaching?

◆ How can I apply what I have learned to help my students?

◆ What more do I want to read, study, or discuss with colleagues?

Teacher Study Group: Action

Teacher study groups can focus on a variety of actions, but actions should revolve around student learning. Common study group actions include:

◆ reading professional books, articles, or journals together

◆ analyzing student data to determine the best instructional practices or student strengths and needs

◆ studying possible solutions to common problems both in the classroom and throughout the school

◆ study to gain endorsement, college, or inservice credit

◆ study to target an action research project

◆ evaluation of a current program or one that may be implemented

Teacher Study Group: Final Action Steps

One of the most important steps for a teacher study group is to always leave with a plan of action.

◆ What data or resources, both formal and informal, will be collected by members?

◆ How will the data or resources be used to further study?

◆ Who is responsible for planning the next meeting?

◆ What books, artifacts, or articles are needed as resources?

◆ Is there anyone who should be contacted to supplement the study?

◆ How will members reflect on learning and report on their new perspectives?

◆ What actions need to be taken in between meetings?

Once study groups become a systemic part of the school culture for teachers, administrators, and students, engagement will be a natural outcome of the immersion in learning.

Demonstrating Learning

I am not a teacher; I am an awakener.

—Robert Frost

She has wrapped up the unit on mixture equations, and moved on to the next subject in her algebra gibberish curriculum. She has spent the entire period lecturing on a new species of mathematical mystery called Linear Systems in Two Variables. She has filled up a world-record three entire blackboards with rules, examples, and solutions for graphing and unraveling these profound puzzles. She is now waving another large piece of chalk around like a pioneer trying to fend off a bear with a bowie knife and saying, "So I hope you all see that solving a system of equations consists of finding all the ordered pairs, if any, which satisfy each of the equations in the system."

—David Klass, author of young adult novel *You Don't Know Me*

Many excellent teachers are brilliant in their content areas, but they have trouble transferring their knowledge to students because they don't model what they know. Telling students *what* to do cannot replace showing them *how* to do it. The old adage *show, don't tell* would be apt advice for teachers whose goal is to foster deep learning in all their students.

Brian Cambourne (1995) notes that demonstration, much like immersion, is "the ability to observe (see, hear, witness, experience, feel, study, explore) actions and artifacts" (85). In good elementary classrooms, demonstration is a natural part of learning. Children experience the joys of reading by listening to their teacher's voice transform words into magical escapes. They watch their teacher manipulate letters into meaning on the board before attempting writing themselves. They even participate in demonstrations by providing the content for the morning news while their teacher makes it visible. By the time students get to middle and high school, however, this pattern of learning is abandoned in favor of a more regimented system of blocked learning segments, seating charts that control social interaction, and a syllabus that predetermines units of study. A chapter is assigned, comprehension questions are answered, content is discussed, a test is given, grades are recorded, and teachers check off having covered the standards. Then, it's on to the next chapter or unit for a replay of the "learning" scenario.

As teachers come to understand the power of demonstration as the infusion of knowledge and skills intertwined with the artifacts and actions of learning, they begin to rethink learning itself. In secondary classes, students actually can become a part of the demonstration as they incorporate what is being demonstrated into their own schema, the compilation of all the experiences and knowledge that they possess.

Perhaps one of the best examples of high school demonstration learning is the driver's education class. Students are given an authentic text—a driver's manual; a meaningful purpose—studying to get their licenses; and are physically placed into the object of the learning, surrounded by it, as it were, while watching teachers and classmates negotiate the very learning they want to master. Even the grade means more than a mark on a report card; it is the ticket to passing the driving test, to say nothing of saving a few hundred dollars on insurance rates.

Why, then, is driver's ed class taught so differently from other subjects that will equally affect the future lives of learners? Why are so many traditional secondary classes stuck in a pattern of learning that excludes demonstration, and how can teachers effectively incorporate this essential condition for learning into their daily practice?

Demonstrating Through Thinking Aloud

One popular instructional technique for teaching reading is thinking aloud, a practice used by teachers to demonstrate how they, as experienced readers, unlock the text by talking through what they are thinking as they read. For example, an English teacher may read the section of Edward Bloor's *Tangerine*, where a sinkhole is enveloping a portable classroom at a middle school, and make comments aloud such as, "I wonder what it feels like to have the earth suddenly disappear. How does Paul know where to run?" The teacher would also demonstrate the natural interaction with vocabulary: "The word the author uses to describe the sudden collapse of the building is *whoosh*. That is such a perfect word! It really sounds like the suction that is taking place as the building begins to fall into the sinkhole. I wonder how the author came up with that word." By eavesdropping on the process effective readers employ as they read, students witness a demonstration that allows them to become aware of themselves as readers, utilizing the same metacognative strategies as the effective teacher reader.

Similarly, content-area teachers can allow students to witness a demonstration of how learners think through difficult text. Following is an example of a teacher thinking aloud with a paragraph from a world history textbook, *Journey Across Time* (Spielvogel 2005, 172).

TEXT: Plato was from a noble Greek family and had planned a career in politics.

TEACHER: I wonder what Plato's family did to be considered noble. I also wonder what a career in politics meant in 375 B.C. Could it be anything like a career in politics today?

TEXT: However, he was so horrified by the death of his teacher, Socrates, that he spent many years traveling and writing.

TEACHER: I want to find out more about how Socrates died. I believe he was murdered, but I'm not sure. Why did he die?

TEXT: When Plato returned to Athens in 387 B.C., he founded an academy, where he taught using Socrates' method of questioning.

TEACHER: What was that method? I know that some teachers use Socratic circles in as a way to get students to question and discuss. I wonder if the present day concept is really similar to what Socrates did.

TEXT: Plato looked for truth beyond the appearances of everyday objects and reflected this philosophy in his writing and teaching. He believed the human soul was the connection between the appearance of things and ideas.

TEACHER: I'll have to think about this. "The human soul was the connection between the appearance of things and ideas." What does he

mean by the *appearance* of things and ideas? What truth was he look-
ing for? I will have to do more research about Plato's ideas to fully
understand what this means.

It is important to demonstrate the process of learning to students so
they can practice thinking through ideas instead of parroting back answers. Students could easily ace a comprehension test on the above paragraph by answering questions such as:

What type of family was Plato from?

On what did Plato base his academy?

What was Plato's philosophy?

Answers are easy; thinking beyond the questions is not. Demonstrate
to students the complex, circular nature of real learning and show them
that comprehension doesn't always mean that you have all the answers. In
fact, it often means that you are just beginning to find the questions.

This concept of thinking aloud can be applied to all classroom learning and teaching. Before a topic is introduced, teachers should demonstrate their own pedagogical thinking by asking themselves the following
questions about the unit and topic. Sharing the questions with the class is
a powerful way of modeling how problem solving or beginning a task is an
ongoing process that requires thinking, questioning, and sometimes even
revising the original plan.

◆ Why am I asking the students to study this chapter, unit, or lesson?

◆ How will this learning enrich the lives of students or help them with
   other school tasks?

◆ How can I demonstrate this learning so students can experience it
   instead of merely reading or hearing about it?

◆ How have I allowed for student exploration of the topic instead of
   passive infiltration?

Demonstrating the process of learning rather than teaching chunks of
information should be best practice in secondary classes where teachers
are struggling to cover more and more content each year. The focus on
teaching literacy skills in content areas may be frustrating to content-
area teachers, but it is a perfect opportunity to demonstrate to students
how to access difficult content-area text. Once students discover how to

comprehend critical vocabulary and complicated text, they will become better content-area students. By demonstrating how literacy skills are a scaffold for content, teachers can provide students with the necessary tools for lifelong learning in every subject.

Demonstrating Vocabulary Use

> Words can almost, sometimes, in moments of grace, attain the quality of deeds.
>
> —Elie Wiesel

Think about how you learn new words or how you may have developed a specialized vocabulary, perhaps related to a hobby or sport. When I read, I write words I don't know on the inside back cover of my book and ask someone who may know them, such as my husband, who has a great vocabulary and is often close by when I am reading. If he's not around, I usually look up the words in a dictionary. Sometimes I am familiar with the word; I just don't remember what it means or I can't figure out a different meaning in a new context. I become frustrated when I look up a word and then a few months later encounter it again but can't remember its meaning. It takes using the word many times in various contexts for me to "own" the word and have it as a permanent part of my vocabulary. Words often drop completely out of my vocabulary and have to be re-placed several times. Explain to your students how you learn new words and the difficulties you encounter in your own vocabulary acquisition.

Demonstrating the use of vocabulary is a far more effective way to help students enlarge their vocabularies than asking them to look up and memorize definitions. Discuss words with students; encourage them to wallow in words by brainstorming possible uses of words and playing around with them. Approach word study as an ongoing practice that will benefit students whether they are planning to go to college or embark on a career after graduation. It is important for students to work in groups to foster discussions about the relationship among words, especially those that represent deeper concepts. Allow students to demonstrate their own knowledge of words by offering a variety of methods for vocabulary study, such as word illustrations, concept word maps, or word charts.

Cover the wall with large sheets of butcher paper and have students write new words they encounter on the chart or post words they may need to know for a new unit of study. Make this a student-friendly, interactive wall by encouraging students to write their own definitions, illustrate the words, or glue pictures from magazines that show the word in action. Once you have identified words that students don't know, create vocabulary activities that help them learn new words.

◆ Have students write several related words from the chart on index cards and then sort or group the words based on the connections among the words.

◆ Have students write synonyms or antonyms from the chart on sticky notes and place them on a wall several feet from each other either in a vertical or horizontal line. Students will come up with other words that are closely related to the two words; write them on new sticky notes and place them between the two words already on the wall. For example:

gregarious giddy joyful mellow quiet subdued **solemn**

◆ Have students write related words on strips of paper and then link them together in a word chain based on their relationship to each other. This is especially helpful for kinesthetic learners.

◆ Have students who understand conceptually important words with broad and multiple meanings such as *capitalism, loyalty*, or *evolution* lead small group discussions about the word.

◆ Use word charts to assess a class' background knowledge of a topic by writing key words related to the topic on the chart and having students place a red dot on words they know well, yellow dots on words they have heard before, and green dots on words that are new to them.

◆ Have students choose a word from the word wall and develop a deeper understanding of the word by writing questions about it and interviewing other students, teachers, or parents about their interpretation of the word. This demonstrates the complexity of the English language by showing students how words are tags for thought.

Demonstrating Text Comprehension

> Why are we reading if not in hope of beauty laid bare, life heightened, and its deepest mystery probed?
>
> —ANNIE DILLARD

A host of professional books and internet sites offer strategies to enhance students' comprehension. Some of these strategies even have names, such as think-pair-share, and others are commonsense instructional techniques that have new and improved packaging. These techniques can certainly be useful for students in helping them untangle inconsiderate text, but their real value lies in *demonstrating* to students how these strategies can be used as tools to help them when they are stuck. For example, show students in content-area classes how you—as a reader, not an expert—might use a graphic organizer or two-column notes to help you make sense of difficult text, especially in science and social studies, for example, and then allow them to create an organizer that best fits their learning needs. Establish specific purposes for students as they begin to read, help them find connections between what they know and what they are learning, and encourage expressions of understanding through a variety of assignments that can be shared with other members of the class.

The Content-Area Circle

Content-area circles are good ways to facilitate authentic, socially constructive ways of comprehending key concepts, unfamiliar vocabulary, or dense text. Have students read a section, topic, or chapter from young adult literature, a content-area textbook, or supplemental text source. In place of comprehension questions or assigned projects, allow students to participate in a guided discussion of the material, much like a study group or literature circle. Demonstrate each of the roles and engage the class in a whole class content-area circle before separating students into groups. The circles are infinitely flexible—depending upon the text, teachers may provide guided questions or prompts or allow free discussion based upon students' responses to the text. Depending on the task, students can turn in detailed notes or forms that the teacher has created for them, or students may only report the highlights of their discussion to the class.

Roles in the Content-Area Circle   Have students choose roles, such as *facilitator, vocabulary finder, researcher, artist, recorder,* and *reporter.* They should be free to come up with other roles that are pertinent to the topic or their purpose. Demonstrate the purpose of each role with the entire class. It may take much of the semester for students to become proficient in their roles, but they will learn by doing.

Facilitator

◆ Prompts the discussion with opened-ended questions or uses a guide that the teacher has provided.

◆ Makes sure everyone has a chance to speak.

◆ Keeps the discussion objective and focused.

◆ Strives to take the group deeper by eliciting responses to comments.

Vocabulary Finder

◆ Records words the group doesn't understand or concepts that need clarification.

◆ Finds meanings of words and explanations of concepts.

◆ Elicits the teacher's help in explaining meanings of words.

Researcher

◆ Uses online, library, or human resources to provide additional information based on the text or the discussion.

◆ Brings in articles or artifacts to deepen discussion or answer questions.

Artist

◆ Draws illustrations or diagrams to enhance meaning of text.

◆ Finds published art that makes a connection to the text.

◆ Creates graphic organizer (with group's input) to clarify text..

Recorder

◆ Keeps careful notes or fills out the answers to questions that the teacher has provided.

◆ Writes a summary of the discussion to give to the teacher.

◆ Provides notes to the group through email or by supplying a paper copy.

Reporter

◆ Presents the group's findings to the rest of the class.

◆ Provides any significant findings to the school newspaper, other teachers and students, or local media.

Although the teacher's role is to offer support and encouragement, provide guiding questions or instruction sheets if necessary, and monitor the progress of the groups, the teacher should keep in mind that the main goal of content-area circles is to build community and transfer ownership of learning to students. As vital components of engagement and motivation, content-area circles demonstrate to students their own ability to learn.

Demonstrating Writing

Writing is a kind of pain I can't do without.

—ROBERT PENN WARREN

It may be difficult for many secondary teachers to demonstrate the art of writing if they are not comfortable with writing themselves. Assigning a cogent prompt for an essay is one thing, but demonstrating how to translate thoughts into a polished essay is quite another. Teachers often fall into the five-paragraph essay trap because such a formula produces a final product that resembles real writing. Unfortunately, the result is sometimes little more than a stylized graphic organizer with paragraphs. Teachers at most levels of writing proficiency can be of more help to students than any canned formula for writing.

Demonstrate the process of writing, whether or not you are an accomplished writer, by showing students how you would approach an essay or writing prompt. You may ask students to help you by having one team create an engaging introduction, another group form the essential points they will cover in the body, and a final group put together a conclusion. In groups or individually, with highlighters in hand, have students answer the following question about the sample writing piece.

◆ Does the essay make sense? If not, highlight anything that is confusing.

◆ What part of the piece is best? Why?

◆ What part needs the most work? Why?

◆ Is there any part that could use additional details or explanation?

◆ If this is in response to a prompt, does the essay sufficiently and clearly addresses the prompt?

◆ Is the essay well organized? Does it flow smoothly from one part to the next?

◆ Does the introduction grab your attention?

◆ Does the conclusion leave you with a sense of closure?

◆ What else would you like to know?

◆ Highlight any spelling or grammatical errors to help the writer begin the editing process.

Collect the students' comments and review them. The next day, demonstrate in front of the class how you would revise your piece, or allow the student authors to do the same with their own writing. Engaging students in your own struggles as a writer and asking them to reverse roles with you demonstrates much more than the writing process—students will see the task from an entirely different perspective. In addition, this exercise demonstrates that you trust your students to be fair, honest, and respectful. You are showing them that although learning can sometimes seem scary, members of a society must rely each other to improve and grow. You are, in essence, demonstrating a major component of learning.

Demonstrating Assessment

Education consists mainly in what we have unlearned.

— Mark Twain

Understanding the role of assessment is a difficult task these days, both for students and teachers. While good teachers assess continuously through observation and conversation, as well as formally, the very nature of assessment has taken on an eerie glow. The stakes are high, the consequences severe, and the process surreal. How can you help students survive testing? Ask yourself the following questions:

1. Why do you assess your students?

2. How often do you assess?

3. What do you assess?

4. How do your students view assessment?

5. What happens to the assessment once it is complete?

6. Do you use various forms of assessment?

7. Does your assessment guide your instruction?

8. Do you use assessment to know both the strengths and needs of your students?

9. Do you use assessment to individualize instruction?

10. Does assessment accurately reflect what your students know?

Demonstrate how to deconstruct test items instead of inundating students with practice tests. Go through sample test items together and show students how you would arrive at an answer. Explain that assessment is a form of learning, a tool to inform you, the teacher, of your students' strengths and areas of need so you can do a better job of helping them learn.

Many school districts, while still mandating semester exams for secondary students, now offer alternative assessments in lieu of pen-and-paper tests. Create an atmosphere that allows students many opportunities to demonstrate what they know, both formally and informally. When assessment is authentic, relevant, and meaningful, student demonstrations will provide still one more opportunity for extending the learning of everyone in the class—teacher and students alike. Below are examples of alternative assessments:

◆ oral presentations, such as a persuasive speech advocating one historical political stance over another in a social studies class, panel discussions, or debates

◆ plays summarizing the events of a short story

◆ videotapes of learning that may have taken place outside of class, such as students showing their work during a science experiment or history fair project

◆ learning logs or response journals kept while reading textbooks or supplemental materials

◆ portfolio of artifacts demonstrating math competence, for example, through graphs, charts, or more complex problems

◆ artistic representation of learning or political cartoons

◆ research projects, utilizing technology if appropriate

◆ interviews with someone knowledgeable in the area of study

◆ conferences in which students discuss their learning challenges and strengths

◆ creative writing incorporating new learning

As for standardized testing, tell students the best preparation for any standardized test is to become actively engaged in the processes of reading, writing, and thinking about a wide variety of topics in relevant and meaningful ways. Then show them that you believe what you are saying by refusing to waste precious learning time passing out test prep materials. John Guthrie's research on factors that affect standardized reading scores shows that 40 percent is reading ability, 20 percent is motivation, 10 percent is format, and 15 percent is error (Guthrie and Alvermann 1999). Most test preparation concentrates on format, and, worse, kills motivation for reading. A few days before the test, show students the format and logistics of the test, try to calm their anxiety, and encourage them to view the test-taking experience as an opportunity to show what they know.

Demonstrating the Joys of Reading

Read in order to live.

—Gustave Flaubert

Teachers who talk to students about what they are reading are demonstrating the importance of reading in their own lives. Bring in copies of your weekend read and share a passage or paragraph. Students are fascinated when you share your own reading secrets—the fact that you that loved reading *Siddhartha* as a college student but hated *The Scarlet Letter* when you were in high school. Book talks will hook even the most reluctant reader, especially when the book talker uses props to help students visualize the text. Encourage students to book talk as well, and create a book-talk circuit among interested teachers who exchange classes for a few minutes for the purpose of sharing a book they have read. Among the many resources on the web, http://booktalkingcolorado.ppld.org/Scripts/DinosamTips.asp has great tips on giving successful book talks. Following are examples of novels conducive to book talks with students.

Fifteen Books That Beg to Be Book Talked

Breathing Underwater by Alex Flinn   This novel that examines an abusive relationship between a high school boy and girl. Recommended for reading and elective classes (life management) and counselors' study book groups.

Ender's Game by Orson Scott Card   Science fiction at its best, involving military genius and a game that could save the world from total destruction. Recommended for science and technology classes.

Fallen Angels by Walter Dean Myers   Two boys just out of high school end up in the Vietnam War. This novel contains strong visual imagery and language but paints a realistic picture of the horrors of war. Recommended for high school U.S. history and English classes.

Gathering Blue by Lois Lowry   Companion to the *The Giver*, this futuristic novel examines the role of a disabled young girl who must make choices that require courage, wisdom, and heart. Recommended for art, ESE, and language arts classes.

Holes by Louis Sachar   The main character is sent to a boys' detention center where he finds all types of exciting adventures. This novel will grab any reader! Recommended for reading classes, middle school language arts, and science classes.

I Am the Cheese by Robert Cormier   This classic novel unwinds its threads in a complex narrative strand that leaves the reader wondering what is real and what is imagined. Recommended for U.S. government and English classes.

Into the Wild by Jon Krakauer   A true story of a young man who hitchhiked into the Alaskan wilderness and never came out. Recommended for geography, history, and English classes.

Maus: A Survivor's Tale by Art Spiegelman   A new form of reading reminiscent of comic books, this graphic novel will hook even the most reluctant readers. Recommended for reading, English, history, and art classes.

Nightjohn by Gary Paulsen   A twelve-year-old slave learns to read from an adult slave. An easy to read, short book full of power and pain. Recommended for middle school history, language arts, and reading classes.

No More Dead Dogs by Gordon Korman   This hilarious account of a student who gets in trouble for telling the truth to his English teacher about a book he hates will delight middle schoolers. Recommended for middle school language arts, drama, and reading classes.

Rising Tiger by Kate DiCamillo   This short tale appeals to readers of all ages: a boy whose mother has died, a girl who doesn't fit in, and, magically, a tiger. Full of figurative language, recommended for all English classes.

Speak by Laurie Halse Anderson   This novels that reflects the harsh realities of high school life for students who struggle to conform. Destined to become a classic. Recommended for secondary English and psychology classes and counselors' book study groups.

Tangerine by Edward Bloor   Set in Florida, this book's main character, Paul Fisher, must come to terms with the natural phenomenon of his new home and the secrets of his past. Contains exciting sports passages. Recommended for PE, English, geography, and reading classes.

Tears of a Tiger by Sharon Draper   A horrible accident leaves Andy unable to forgive himself and causes him to examine his own future. A favorite among all readers. Recommended for reluctant readers.

You Don't Know Me by David Klass   This first-person narrative leaves the reader laughing and crying at once. This story of a fourteen-year-old who is physically abused by the man who is to become his stepfather has been described as having "magical realism." Readers of all ages will connect with the main character and his zany friends. This book has great passages about math, uses vocabulary in new ways, and would be perfect for counselors' group study.

Engaging English Language Learners (ELL)

Students who are struggling with English can learn much from other students by watching, listening, and actively engaging in the process of learning. The more demonstrative learning that takes place in a class, the better chance the ELL student will have of catching on. Teaching by demonstration is inherently appealing to the ELL student because of the wide variety of visual, auditory, and kinesthetic "clues" that enhance comprehension. Provide regular opportunities for ELL students to demonstrate what they know instead of merely relegating them to paper-and-pen drills, techniques that have been proven unsuccessful with ELL students. As all teachers know, the way to truly learn something is to teach it. Allow

ELL students to practice being teachers on their journeys to becoming better learners.

Demonstrating Learning: Study Groups for Teachers

In business, good ideas lead to increased profit, and workers are rewarded monetarily or given promotions as an incentive for sharing them. Unfortunately, teachers' good ideas often remain behind closed doors or are shared with only a small group of colleagues. A teacher study group is a perfect way to uncap the energy surrounding teachers and to put their innovative practices to work for all students.

Teacher Study Group: Reflection

Think about something you do well in the classroom, a resource or practice that has proven successful for you and your students. Topics may include:

- classroom management
- discussion techniques
- content-area units
- supplemental resources
- technology
- flexible grouping
- alternative assessment
- writing
- handling the paper load

Write or think about when you have used the practice, idea, or tool most successfully and under what circumstances it could be used by others.

Teacher Study Group: Action

In groups of six or fewer, members will demonstrate their area of expertise to others in the group, one demonstration per meeting. If possible, the demonstrating teacher will provide an artifact along with the demonstration, such as a videotape of the practice or students engaged in learning, an article or book that addresses the practice, teacher observational notes, student work samples, or written instructions for utilizing the practice.

Teacher Study Group: Final Action Steps

Group members will reunite after the final session and report on their challenges and successes using the shared ideas, allowing opportunities for refining practices based on experiences and reflection. Consider demonstrating especially effective or instructional techniques to the faculty or at conferences.

5

Expecting Learning

No pessimist ever discovered the secrets of
the stars, or sailed to an uncharted land, or
opened a new heaven to the human spirit.

—HELEN KELLER

Reflecting on Expectations

We all have expectations. Those who are more pessimistically oriented expect war, famine, and locusts, not necessarily in that order. Others greet the day with unrealistically high expectations despite finding a flock of locusts on their front porch. If you have never thought about expectations in terms of optimism or pessimism, you may also not be aware of their importance in your teaching life. Because expectations gauge how you view the world and, to some degree, dictate the events that happen in your life, it is important not only to examine your own expectations but also to be aware of how they are mirrored to students. Ask yourself the following questions:

◆ Think back to the last time you had a negative or positive expectation for an event, interaction, or occurrence.

What was the event?

What was your prediction or expectation?

Did your expectation turn out to be accurate, better than expected, or worse than expected?

- Do others describe you as an encourager or tell you that you always expect the worst?

- Choose one student in your class and think about that student in terms of your expectations for him or her.

  How do you expect the student to behave in class tomorrow?

  What do you expect his or her grade to be at the end of the grading period?

  Do you expect the student to attend college?

  What career do you expect the student to have?

  Do you expect this student to be successful in life?

- Do you believe that your expectations of others can influence their behavior and chances of success?

- Are your students aware of your expectations for them personally and academically?

- What are your expectations for yourself?

Most good teachers will tell you that they know it is important to have high expectations for their students. They are aware of research that shows how expectations can actually change the performance, attitude, and behavior of students. The same student will perform differently for a teacher who expects him to do well than for a teacher who has low expectations. Our own experiences bear out this principle; we all remember a parent, teacher, or coach who believed in us and knew we were able to achieve more than we believed possible. We may also remember an experience when someone doubted or ridiculed our abilities and the resultant fear or doubt crippled our performance. There is little worse than being cast in a negative concrete expectation that leaves little hope of breaking out of the mold. Expectations are both powerful motivators and commanding deterrents.

The effect of this self-fulfilling prophecy is that a student's performance or behavior is directly influenced by a teacher's expectations. A teacher's judgment—positive or negative—is closely related to a student's motivation and self-confidence, both necessary components for his or her success. This same theory applies to parental expectations; their beliefs can significantly affect their child's development, abilities, and capabilities. As Brian Cambourne wrote, "Expectations are subtle and powerful coercers of behavior" (1995, 187). Having high expectations for students goes beyond a superficial statement such as, "I know that you can succeed."

Students are savvy and can accurately interpret attitudes, nonverbal clues, intonation, and actions. Teachers who believe that students are born with a fixed intelligence send out invisible signals, much like laser rays, that pierce students, convincing them that they are incapable of rising above some sort of predetermined intellectual ceiling. The truth is that intelligence is fluid and malleable and responds to a variety of factors, including motivation, interest, readiness, and emotion. James Zull notes in *The Art of Changing the Brain:*

> Teaching is the art of changing the brain. I don't mean controlling the brain, or rearranging it according to some "brain manual." I mean, *creating conditions that lead to change in a learner's brain.* We can't get inside and rewire a brain, but we can arrange things so that it gets rewired. If we are skilled, we can set up conditions that favor this rewiring, and we can create an environment that nurtures it. (2002, 5)

Expecting that students can and will learn is a first step in creating an environment that nurtures learning. Cambourne is clear, however, that such expectations cannot exist without a genuine relationship between the student and teacher. The message should be unequivocal from teacher to student: I like you, I have confidence in your abilities, and I value you. I care about your accomplishments, no matter how small, and I see you as a person, not just a student who happened to be assigned to my class.

Forming Realistic Expectations About Students

> Vanessa, who can barely read or write, really likes learning the sign language alphabet. She is very proud that she can spell her name with it. I told her that she could teach the deaf someday.
>
> —ESME RAJI CODELL, *EDUCATING ESME*

Often classroom teachers have too many students in one class and too many classes in one day. If schools are on the block schedule and teachers have students only for one semester, they may have difficulty remembering names, coming to know students as individuals, or even distinguishing between one student and another. Teachers feel they have little choice—hold back the sea of students or drown. The idea of differentiating instruction, teaching to meet individual needs, or forming accurate expectations seems an unrealistic task. Since it is literally impossible to form positive expectations of students without knowing the real person behind the pierced nose, dyed hair, or cheerleader outfit, teachers must spend time forming relationships at every opportunity, and they must ensure that class members know each other as well, not as a collective whole but as individuals. Because all learning is social, it is important to set the stage for students to become interdependent, relying on themselves and each other, as well as the teacher, as they learn.

Expecting Students to Be Individuals

One way to establish such an environment is to have students complete a booklet about themselves as one of the first assignments in your class. Give students a week or more to finish the project at home, and let them know that their writings will be shared with the entire class or in small groups, unless they request otherwise. Teachers should respond to the final product in a noncritical, conversational, authentic manner, in writing or orally, by utilizing a variety of methods such as a cassette tape, talking with the student in a conference setting, or through email. It is best not to grade the booklet, but instead mark it with a completion grade to foster a climate of engagement and trust. Following is an example of how students might create booklets.

Student Booklet Instructions

Design a cover that reflects you. Consider a collage of magazine pictures, a poem, an illustration, graphic art, or photographs. The cover will be displayed on the wall of the classroom for other students to peruse.

Choose any three of the following essay topics to include in your booklet.

◆ Write a complete reading history, including favorite books, when and where you like to read, how you became a reader, and what type of exposure you have had to reading. Include positive and negative school reading experiences.

◆ How do you view the subject of _____ (math, science, social studies, English). Has this subject traditionally been easy or difficult for you? Are you interested in learning a specific area of the subject? What experiences have you had in other grades that influenced your attitude toward this subject?

◆ Write a short autobiography, including interesting experiences, anec-
dotes, and recollections from your past, or write a chronological outline
of your life so far. Have your parent or guardian include a paragraph
about what kind of kid you were, if you like.

◆ Write about your future, your short-term and long-term plans for a job
or career, your leisure time activities, and your hobbies. You might
write about what you would like to do with your life, even if it seems
impractical or farfetched, such as playing pro football, becoming a
famous singer, or joining the Peace Corps.

◆ Write a list of twenty-five things you don't think you could live without.
Be specific and add details by way of explanation.

◆ Describe in detail your family members and/or best friends, including
specifically what you like about each. Include pictures if you wish.
Remember to show and not simply tell. Give examples of each person's
behavior and characteristics.

◆ Write about a person or people who have shaped your life so far. These
might be personal friends, mentors, or famous people who have influenced you from afar.

◆ Write a personal essay about an experience you've had that is especially funny, unique, sad, embarrassing, or memorable.

◆ Write about a pet peeve you have or a philosophy you have developed
about life.

Expecting More Than High Test Scores

> Psychometric scientists agree that it is unscientific to use a single
> test performance to make decisions about individuals, including
> decisions about grade promotion or retention and about what a
> child knows, what needs to be taught, and how to teach it.
>
> —RICHARD ALLINGTON

Although creating an atmosphere of high expectations for each student
is the rhetoric behind many state and federal initiatives, specifically for
reading, it is difficult to achieve that goal when the school or district
focuses all of its resources, time, and energy on having students pass a
single life-altering test. The stories become more disheartening with each
passing year:

◆ A high school band room, like a relic from the past with risers and practice studios, has been transformed into a computer lab for the purpose of putting all students through a computer testing program. Where do kids practice their instruments? The question is unnecessary; there is no longer a band program.

◆ A teacher for more than twenty years who has been immensely successful teaching students with special needs, perhaps because he himself was a kid with specials need, quits because he can't stand seeing his students spend every moment practicing for a test that they are unlikely to pass. "They'll quit, too," he said. "Why should they stay in school and fail?"

◆ A teacher in Texas blows the whistle. The administrator is encouraging the staff to help students cheat on the standardized test. Why? So everyone from the superintendent to the classroom teacher will receive a performance bonus.

◆ A summer enrichment program is discontinued in favor of "summer remediation." Art, PE, music, and vocational classes in schools throughout the nation are tossed away like yesterday's trash. Why waste time in physical, practical, or aesthetic endeavors? Every spare moment is devoted to test preparation.

◆ Students who look forward to taking a field trip to see the play *The Miracle Worker* in conjunction with their study of Helen Keller find that the trip has been cancelled. All field trips are prohibited before testing dates.

◆ The school's library budget is cut, money is not available for supplemental materials, and copy paper is in short supply. Closets full of booklets containing isolated practice tests have taken the place of authentic learning materials.

These true stories are only the tip of a very deep and dangerous iceberg. Ask any teacher or student and they will report equally tragic stories. The expectation for students has been reduced to a simple mantra: *pass the test.* From the first day of school until the day of the test in the spring, students are threatened, coerced, and test-prepped almost to the point of catatonia. Learning has taken a backseat in a breakneck race to be the best school in the district, have the highest score in the school, or gain extra bonus money for high performance. Frustrated and discouraged, teachers themselves are disengaged amid testing hysteria. In a state-level curriculum meeting about how to raise test scores, one outspoken teacher shouted, "Testing is not a subject!" Testing is not learning, either. It is vitally important to establish an atmosphere where the expectation is for learning, not high scores on a standardized test. Ironically, when students are engaged in learning, their chances of scoring well on a standardized test are much greater than if they spend the year completing practice test items. The casualties of the current testing insanity will be evident for many years to come.

Refuse to play the testing game. Show students from the very first day that you expect more from them than a high score on a standardized test. Find research such as studies in *Engaged Reading* (Guthrie and Alvermann 1999) that "being a wide and frequent reader increases a student's reading achievement by 10-15 percentile points on standard tests" (17) and prove it through your own action research. Keep a journal of your teaching practices and student comments, as well as a sampling of creative and academic student work. Then, turn your artifacts into an article that demonstrates what is possible in a class where a teacher dares to do the right thing for her students. Submit your article to national organizations or state affiliates in your content area or a professional organization such as:

National Council of Teachers of English: www.ncte.org

National Council of Teachers of Mathematics: www.nctm.org

National Council for the Social Studies: www.ncss.org

National Science Teachers Association: www.nsta.org

National Staff Development Council: www.nsdc.org

International Reading Association: www.reading.org

Association for Supervision and Curriculum Development: www.ascd.org

Creating a culture of high expectations involves more than the classroom teacher. It involves a commitment on the part of the entire school. Such a move may be an evolution from a place where teachers often fall into the habit of speaking sarcastically or negatively about students to a place where students have the right to begin each day with a clean slate and the assurance of their own abilities. The school's leadership team should address this issue with as much thought and determination as they put into the school improvement plan, next year's curriculum, or textbook selection. None of the school's exterior window dressing or fancy mission statements will make attractive a school that is diseased from within by constant negativity or disrespect of students. How does a school begin a renaissance from the inside?

Setting Schoolwide Expectations

1. Send out surveys to students and teachers gauging the *expectation quotient* of the school. (See the Teacher Study Group guide at the end of this chapter for a sample survey.)

2. In a faculty meeting, set guiding principles for improving the atmosphere of the school. For example:

    ◆ All conversations about students will be held in confidence between the parties involved.

    ◆ As much as possible, students will be involved in any conferences about behavior, attitude, performance, or disruptive incidents.

    ◆ Faculty members will make a conscious effort to set high expectations for students in each class and verbalize these expectations often.

    ◆ Students will be encouraged to set their own learning and behavioral goals as a way of reinforcing the importance of personal expectations.

    ◆ Students will not be labeled or sorted by standardized test scores; rather the value of the individual will be determined by who he is, not how he performs on a test.

3. Create opportunities for acknowledging each student's contribution to the school or class community, no matter how small.

4. Create an advisory mentoring program whereby each student is known individually by a faculty member who appreciates his or her individual talents and abilities.

5. Address the problems of students who are dealing with motivation or self-esteem issues by forming study or discussion groups with pertinent young adult or bibliotherapy books that allow students to adjust their own expectations.

We must believe in our ability to stretch our students' learning and we must believe in their ability to learn beyond any textbook, test, or curriculum. We must believe that they are artists who are imminently capable of creating something more beautiful and significant than anything we can imagine.

Expectations for English Language Learners (ELL)

English Language Learners are often bright, interesting, and talented students who have much to offer because their experiences have given them a depth of background knowledge. Instead of expecting these students to look, speak, and act like every other student in the school, allow them to celebrate their differences by sharing their knowledge and experiences with class members. Help them form positive expectations for themselves by getting to know them and guiding them in their areas of strength as well as helping them with their challenges. Tragically, many students who read perfectly well in their own language are placed in intensive reading classes and put through phonics drills or low-level comprehension questioning. They then fall behind their classmates. Expectations for these students means giving them the opportunity to show what they know and allowing them to share this knowledge with their teachers and classmates.

Expectations for Learning: Study Groups for Teachers

Teacher Study Group: Reflection

Consider the expectations of various groups within the school. In writing or as a group discussion, reflect on the following:

- students' expectations for themselves
- teachers' expectations for themselves
- students' expectations of other students
- teachers' expectations of students

Teacher Study Group: Action

Have each group member come back with qualitative data in the form of words, phrases, or actions that relate to expectations. Determine the *expectation quotient* of the school by giving a survey such as the following to students, faculty, and/or parents.

1. Do you feel that most of your teachers believe that you will succeed?

2. What are your expectations for yourself?

3. What is expected of you as a student at this school? Check all that apply.

    ☐ to score well on the standardized test

    ☐ to follow the rules

    ☐ to learn as much as I can

    ☐ to excel athletically

    ☐ to find out about myself as a learner

    ☐ to become prepared for college

    ☐ to become prepared for a career

    ☐ to be creative and artistic

    ☐ to find out who I am

    ☐ to become a successful and valued citizen

    ☐ other:

Teacher Study Group: Final Action Steps

Once the study group has a realistic picture of their students' expectations of themselves, the teachers' expectations of students, and the school community's expectations of itself, teachers can begin a meaningful dialogue about how to alter or raise expectations to maximize learning.

6

Responsibility for Learning

The teacher's task is not to implant facts but to place the subject to be learned in front of the learner and, through sympathy, emotion, imagination, and patience, to awaken in the learner the restless drive for answers and insights which enlarge the personal life and give it meaning.

—NATHAN M. PUSEY

Which of the following have you said to students?

◆ With privileges come responsibilities.

◆ Be responsible: Bring your paper, pencil, and book to class.

◆ If you are not responsible with _____ (the computer, group work, free time), then you will lose it.

◆ Because you weren't responsible enough to turn in your homework, you won't be allowed to earn extra credit.

◆ Responsible students have a better chance at scholarships, awards, and favorable letters of recommendation from teachers.

◆ It is your responsibility to get your notebook in order or I will not grade it.

How do our students view responsibility? Is it a stick with which we prod and coerce them into behavior or actions that we wish to see exhibited and that may be, admittedly, good for them? Or do students see the act of being responsible as one that will buy them extrinsic rewards? While responsible behavior may have positive, short-term effects on learning, *true* responsibility involves intrinsic fulfillment. According to Brian

Cambourne, responsibility means that learners make their own decisions about "when, how and what 'bits' to learn in any learning task. Learners who lose the ability to make decisions are disempowered." He makes the point that when very young children begin to talk, they are permitted to make some decisions (i.e., take responsibility) because they are provided with language demonstrations that are not "specially arranged in terms of simple to complex." He points out,

> No one decides beforehand which particular language convention or set of conventions children will attend to and subsequently internalize. Learners are left some choice about what they'll engage with next. Learners are able to exercise this choice because of the consistency of the language demonstrations occurring in the everyday ebb and flow of human discourse. (Cambourne 1995, 185)

Adolescents adhere to much the same principle. Even those who don't spend most of their day around teens know that they are capable of making choices and, in fact, will do so whether we allow them to or not. Many teachers spend their time trying to effect change in their learners instead of empowering them with the responsibility to do so themselves.

Most of us know students who inherently embrace responsibility for their learning, but we also know students whose parents assume that responsibility for them or try desperately to transfer the role to the teacher. Paradoxically, enabling students by assuming the responsibility for their learning disables students in their future endeavors. Just as a moth struggles to free itself from its cocoon, and in so doing becomes strong enough to live, we must allow our students to find and use their own capabilities to accomplish the tasks before them. To open the cocoon and free the moth will doom it to certain death. It is the process, the struggle, that leads to freedom—and to learning.

How does a teacher begin the process of relinquishing responsibility for her students' learning and empowering them to pick up the reins of their own journey? Unlike other professionals, teachers' days are dictated by five or more timed intervals in which they must corral, manage, and increasingly be accountable for the thoughts and actions of groups of people who may be, in varying degrees, immature, unreasonable, mischievous, or hormonal. They must deal with federal, state and district mandates, irrelevant interruptions from blaring loudspeakers, and hall-lunchroom-bathroom-homeroom duties as required by their contracts. It is little wonder that teachers grasp those reins tightly to keep from falling out of the wagon.

It takes courage to let go and transfer responsibility with so many potential pitfalls along the way.

In considering Cambourne's theory that students must make their own decisions about "when, how, and what bits to learn," teachers can start off slowly and gauge their students' reactions and learning. Anne, a teacher at an upscale high school who had been teaching honors English for years, reported that her students were unmotivated to do more than was necessary to earn a good grade. She felt that she was failing to adequately prepare them for college because she couldn't seem to spark that love of learning that had been so important in her own educational development. She reported to the school literacy council, "My students will only do the bare minimum, even though they are bright and capable. I can't get them to do anything more—to experience deep learning." Anne decided to experiment with her instructional techniques to see if she could pinpoint the problem and ended up engaging in an action research project. She had two college dual-enrolled classes with similar demographics, sizes, and abilities. In one class, she instructed the students as she had for several years. She handed out the assignment (related to an exploration of language) and the rubric, placed students in groups, gave them the due date, and provided a list of suggested topics. In the other class, she turned the responsibility of the project over to the students after an initial, open-ended discussion about language. She instructed the students that they were to complete a project that involved the acquisition of language. They were allowed to choose their own groups and time line, but they had to schedule conferences with her to keep her informed of their progress. The requirement remained the same for both groups: an oral and written report.

The results were startling. Although the class that had been given responsibility for its own learning initially experienced cognitive dissonance, that uncomfortable intellectual place where new thinking and ideas have not yet become clarified, the students soon sprang to life. They formed groups on their own, worked after school, moved outside of the parameters of the assignment—in one case studying language development in an elementary class—and met with Anne to get her feedback and advice. Their final products showed a vast amount of research and analysis compared to the group to whom she had given all of the instructions. The experimental groups' projects demonstrated creativity, deep thinking, and an understanding of the data they had collected. Some even created videotapes to enhance their oral projects. Overall, she reported that the class with fewer guidelines far exceeded the other class in attitude toward learning, work ethic, and quality of final product.

Anne said that while her students were learning about language, she was learning about her own teaching. She wasn't sure if the same process would work with other assignments or with other groups of students, but she was convinced that she had taken a step in helping students rediscover the joys so often missing in school learning by allowing the responsibility to be theirs alone.

Discovering Responsibility

I bid you lose me and find yourselves.

—FRIEDRICH WILHELM NIETZSCHE

Cambourne's recommendation that students must decide "when, how, and what bits to learn" doesn't mean curriculum anarchy. What it does mean is that the learner has access to a powerful component of motivation: choice in some aspects of the learning task. Instead of telling students when an assignment is due, for example, consider allowing the class to vote on a due date. Once students get accustomed to this freedom, they will begin to check dates for other class projects or school events, weigh the amount of time the project will take, and learn the critical task of managing their own time. Furthermore, they will learn to take responsibility for late work, since they have no one to blame if they don't meet the deadline. If this approach does not work for your classes, consider providing a form students can fill out requesting additional time on an individual basis. Give students the responsibility for requesting an extended deadline to complete a project or assignment. (See Figure 6.1 for an example of a due date extension form.)

While this process may seem time intensive for the teacher, it really takes far less time than listening to dozens of students explain why an assignment is late or asking if they can have "just one more day" due to a variety of incredible unforeseen circumstances. The bonus for everyone is that students are practicing the skills of thinking through a problem, writing for an authentic purpose, and learning to take responsibility for managing their time.

Many students have not discovered *how* to take responsibility for their own learning because they have not had opportunities to think deeply about issues, form opinions, and analyze contradictory positions. They may have spent their schooling acting as compliant—or not so compliant—vessels into which knowledge is poured by a more

Due Date Extension Form

Assignment _____

Today's Date _____

Original Due Date _____

1. What new due date are you requesting? _____

2. Describe in full detail the work you have done on the assignment so far. Attach a copy of what you have completed if appropriate.

3. Why are you requesting additional time to complete the project or assignment?

4. How many times in the past have you filled out a due date extension form?

5. If the due-date extension is not approved, how do you propose to address this problem?

FIGURE 6.1

knowledgeable one: the teacher, textbook, or learning program. Most learning theories, while differing in specifics, come to one general conclusion: Learning is a social process and it is through interaction with others that knowledge is constructed. Social interaction also leads to increased conceptual understanding across the content areas. This is different from memorizing facts to pass a test—it is the essence of how we learn. Providing opportunities for students to participate in authentic discussion, debate, and deliberation fosters responsibility for learning because they create opportunities for forming, expressing, and owning intellectual thoughts and opinions. When their contributions are valued, students—like adults—come to life. By standing back and allowing students to become reflective, thoughtful learners, the teacher becomes the wise master who does not give the proverbial fish, but instead shows students how to fish for a lifetime.

While not every topic in every subject will lend itself to discussion, and while dialogue takes more time than answering questions at the back of the chapter, the valuable skills of thinking analytically, listening critically to others, and weighing varying views will become internalized as students engage in one of the most basic and satisfying of human undertakings: social interaction through discussion. The following activity provides an opportunity for discussion that will encourage students to think deeply and critically about difficult issues.

1. Guide students in learning how to dialogue, debate, and deliberate by giving them the responsibility for setting ground rules for discussion, such as:

   ◆ Everyone's voice is heard.

   ◆ There will be no ridicule or sarcasm.

   ◆ No one person will dominate the discussion.

   ◆ The facilitator (or teacher) will have the final word.

   ◆ Students will keep notes during the discussion and address points, not personalities.

2. Put students in groups, or let them to choose their groups, but change groups frequently to allow students the opportunity to interact with different classmates. Make sure everyone has a role, such as facilitator, recorder, timekeeper, and so on.

3. Provide essential questions related to the topic of study or keep a box where students may supply relevant and meaningful questions, such as:

   ◆ *English:* In this short story or novel, the main character took an action that some might consider immoral (suicide, theft, lying). Discuss the issue from the point of view of different characters. How do you feel about the character's action? In what ways could it be justified? What is morality?

   ◆ *Science:* Evidence suggests that the polar ice cap is melting. Is global warming a scientifically based position or is this the view of biased environmentalists? What evidence would it take for you to change your position?

   ◆ *Social Studies:* It has been argued that war is a result of one group demanding that others be like them. Discuss the merit of this statement. When, if ever, is war justified? Provide examples to support your argument.

   ◆ *PE:* There has been much discussion about athletes using steroids to enhance their performance. Should athletes be required take drug tests to monitor steroid use?

4. The student recorder should keep notes on chart paper, detailing both sides of the issue.

5. If time permits, allow each group to present a summary of the discussion to the class and elicit their views.

Hopefully, these discussions will continue after class, perhaps even at home. Students will learn to take responsibility for determining and expressing intellectual opinions in a clear, measured way. Such discussions have the potential to spark lifelong interests leading to increased civil responsibility, social tolerance, and an awareness of the multiple facets of most current issues.

Learning to Think

> Reading furnishes the mind only with materials of knowledge; it is thinking that makes what we read ours.
>
> —John Locke

Help students become responsible for *what* they learn by allowing them to read and write something that they want to explore related to the course. Students who read widely are more successful in school, score higher on standardized tests, and have a greater chance of using literacy in their life pursuits. In place of wide reading and relevant application through writing, many content-area teachers spend valuable time taking students through the motions of a formulaic research paper, an often meaningless exercise that takes hours of class time. In this age of information and communication technologies, often called *multiliteracies*, students need to know how to access information, use it to help them gain knowledge or solve problems, and transform it from isolated fragments of information to an interlocking piece of their own schema. By restructuring existing information into relevant knowledge, students are inherently assuming responsibility for learning. Give students the opportunity to experience this intellectual gratification by providing a structure, such as the learning project explored below, to engage them in deep and meaningful reading, writing, and thinking.

A Learning Project

Tell students that they will have the opportunity to read and write about something related to the course. Give them plenty of examples of relevant learning topics and allow time for discussion. Encourage students to think outside the box and gain intrinsic rewards by satisfying their own curiosity.

One of the most challenging aspects of this project will be for students to make a decision about what they will study and form a plan about how they will accomplish their goals. This important process is a natural first step in allowing students to experience the messy work of taking responsibility for their own learning.

Sample Topics for a Content-Area Reading/Writing Project

Literature/Reading

◆ Read the novel *1984* by George Orwell and write a summary of what Orwell predicted life would be like in 1984. Research the events that took place in the year 1984 and compare Orwell's predictions to reality.

◆ Compare a novel or short story by Stephen King to Henry James' *Turn of the Screw* or Edgar A. Poe's short stories. Write about the evolution of ghost stories or write one yourself in the style of one of the writers.

◆ Compare a traditional young adult novel to a graphic novel, such as *Maus*. Write a review of each book, noting the characters, language, and how the illustrations change the reading experience.

Social Studies

◆ Research an event in United States history that you want to know more about. You might delve into recent history by talking with someone who was in New York during the 9/11 attacks or interviewing people who remember the *Challenger* accident or Kent State shootings. You should read accounts from that time period from various sources. Write about the event as if you were a reporter. Approach a local newspaper about publishing your article on the anniversary of the historical event.

◆ What caused the fall of the stock market in 1929 and the ensuing depression? Could it happen today? Read historical accounts of the depression, interview stockbrokers, and make your own predictions.

◆ Read about Shackleton's second expedition to Antarctica or the expedition of Lewis and Clark. Write an account of the trip as if you were a member of the team who accompanied the famous explorers. Consider a journal format.

Science

◆ What is the string theory or Einstein's theory of relativity? How difficult is it to comprehend the theories by reading about them? Write an essay that explains one of the theories in simple language, using drawings or a comic book format if appropriate. Donate your paper to an elementary or middle school science class.

◆ Read about and survey various species of trees, plants, or flowers in a local wetland area. Create a scrapbook of photographs or drawings as well as a written description of the researched plants.

◆ Consider a current topic related to biology such as mad cow disease, bacteriological warfare, or the Ebola outbreak. Describe the factors that characterize these issues. Write about how any one of these occurrences might affect your generation. Submit a short article from your research to the school newspaper.

Use the above as examples to stimulate the thinking of your students, but encourage them to find their own topics. I once had a student who wanted to know more about AIDS. She researched the disease, interviewed a young mother who had contracted AIDS, and presented the information to the class in one of the most moving presentations I have ever seen. I doubt any of those students will ever forget the power of her report, and what they learned that day undoubtedly will stay with them forever.

Planning Form for a Content-Area Reading/Writing Project

Each student should submit the following planning form prior to beginning work on the project.

1. What is the topic of your project?

2. Why did you choose this topic?

3. What do you hope to learn?

4. What challenges do you foresee in completing this project?

5. How will you address these challenges?

6. What will you read related to the topic?

7. What will you write that will reflect what you leaned from your reading, such as a short story, research paper, essay, magazine article, or poetry?

8. What other types of resources do you plan to use, such as interviews, primary-based documents, movies, photographs, music, art?

9. Describe the time line for your project.

◆ When do you plan to have the reading completed?

◆ When will you begin writing, or do you plan to write as you read?

♦ When do you plan to meet with the teacher for a project conference?

On the day that the project is due, have students place their reports and/or visual aids on a table. One or more class periods should be devoted to reading and responding to the projects. Provide index cards or sticky notes so that students can write responses to at least three projects. Return the notes to the writer as a way of providing authentic feedback. Because these reports vary in format, content, topic, and style, and because the work is done by their peers, even reluctant readers will engage in the reading and responding.

Teacher Response to a Content-Area Reading/Writing Project

In grading these projects, your first task is to get outside your role of teacher and respond to the final project as a reader might. Note the points that appeal to you, teach you, amaze you, or confuse you. Put your comments on sticky notes or index cards to preserve the integrity of the project and as a way of modeling what you are asking students to do. Assign three holistic grades: one for the process, one for the written report, and one for the oral presentation, remembering that a major purpose of this assignment is to foster independence, responsibility, and intellectual curiosity. Allow the class to help develop the criteria for grading before the work begins.

Process

♦ Did the student meet with you as planned?

♦ Did the student turn in a planning form and fulfill the requirements of the contract?

♦ Did the student demonstrate evidence of ongoing work, such as taking advantage of available class time, library opportunities, and conferences with you?

Written Product

♦ Does the project deal with the subject in an in-depth manner that demonstrates learning?

♦ Has the student effectively incorporated the outside reading with his or her own thoughts concerning the topic?

♦ Is the project clearly written and easy to read?

◆ What growth do you see in the student's skills, abilities, and knowledge?

◆ Has the student met writers' guidelines for grammar, spelling, and punctuation?

◆ Did the student meet his or her expectations for learning? Did the student meet your expectations?

Oral Report

◆ Is the student knowledgeable about the topic?

◆ Is the presentation organized and easy to understand?

◆ Does the presentation reflect thought, analysis, and a thorough examination of the topic?

◆ Are there visual aids that enhance the report?

Once students experience the flow of being involved in a project of their own making, they will begin to change as learners. The satisfaction of learning and pride in their own accomplishments will act as a magnet that pulls them forward rather than their being pushed from behind by someone who has assumed the responsibility for getting them to move.

Responsibilities for English Language Learners (ELL)

Many students struggling to learn a new language feel that they have been stripped of any efficacy they might have once enjoyed in their own country or culture. In the new world in which they have found themselves, it often becomes the teacher's responsibility to ensure the student learns the content of the class while the student is left to deal with language and cultural barriers. Give these students responsibility for at least some aspect of their learning. Ask them how they learn best and allow learning in different ways. As students set their own learning goals, they should be allowed to experiment with schooling. These students will benefit from an independent reading and writing project because their natural interest will lift them over many of the challenges inherent in a typical classroom setting and the process will increase both the rate and depth of their learning.

While not all teachers will be comfortable giving students increased responsibility, this group provides an opportunity to experiment with the process and come back together to share experiences, successes, and challenges. Much as Anne did when she allowed one group of students to assume responsibility for their project on language acquisition, consider using this study session as an action research project that targets the impact of responsibility on student learning.

Teacher Study Group: Reflection

Engage in a discussion that examines the meaning of responsibility and its role in your school or class. Use the following questions as a springboard for discussion.

◆ To what degree do your students assume responsibility:

for their own learning?

for their lives outside of class?

for going beyond what it takes to get a passing grade?

for turning assignments in on time?

◆ To what degree do you, as teachers, encourage students to assume responsibility by:

discussing with students the concept of responsibility as intrinsic fulfillment?

allowing choices in reading and/or writing assignments?

providing students opportunities to engage in relevant discussions based on their own understanding of the content?

turning over some control of curriculum topics to students?

Teacher Study Group: Action

Choose an assignment or long-term project that students typically complete "just to earn a grade" with little regard for deep learning. Consider ways that you could return responsibility to students by offering choices in any or all of the following:

◆ deadlines based on student need

◆ topics based on student choice

◆   texts based on student interest

◆   products based on student learning styles

◆   discussions based on student-generated questions

◆   writing process or format based on student preference

When students are given responsibility for their own learning, will their engagement, motivation, and quality of work improve?

Once you decide how you will alter your assignment or instructional technique, keep a notebook in which you record observations of student behaviors, reactions, and questions. Use the following questions to help frame your observations.

1. Specifically, how did students react to the assignment? Include comments, questions, actions, attitudes, and body language.

2. What behaviors did you observe during the process in the following areas:

    engagement

    motivation

    interest

    interaction with classmates

    type and frequency of questions addressed to teacher and classmates

    creativity

    critical thinking

3   In what way did you observe that students assumed (or did not assume) responsibility for their own learning?

4. In what way, if any, were the final products different from other assignments or projects completed by these students?

5. How did the process and products from this class compare to a similar class that did not have choice in some form of the learning?

Although this data is not quantitative, it will be valuable in providing objective evidence of how or if releasing responsibility to students affects learning. Give the following reflection survey to students at the end of the research project to measure their perceptions.

1. In what way did having more choice in this assignment affect your learning?

2. Did you procrastinate getting the assignment finished?

3. Did you spend more or less time on this assignment than similar projects in which the teacher set all of the guidelines?

4. How much did you care about this assignment as opposed to others you have done in this class?

5. Do you plan to continue learning about this topic in the future?

6. What was the most valuable aspect of this assignment in terms of your own learning?

7. What, if anything, made you uncomfortable about this assignment?

8. Did you discover anything about yourself as a learner while doing this assignment?

Teacher Study Group: Final Action Steps

Teachers should compile the group's data into an action research notebook on responsibility and place it in the school's professional library. As study groups continue this process on various topics, the notebooks will become a valuable professional resource as well as a record of teachers' ongoing learning.

Using Learning

It is the supreme art of the teacher to awaken
joy in creative expression and knowledge.

—ALBERT EINSTEIN

Consider the following scenarios.

Scenario A

After purchasing a home, you receive a microscopically fonted home-owner's insurance policy with a three-page addendum telling you what to do when filing a claim damage due to a natural disaster, such as hurricane, flood, or fire. What do you do with the document?

A. Read each word and take notes so you will be prepared for a natural disaster.

B. Give the document to your spouse to read.

C. Call the insurance company and ask for a verbal explanation.

D. File the document in your homeowner's insurance policy file.

E. Throw the document in the garbage with a comment that if something happens you will call the insurance company and get another copy.

Scenario B

You experience a natural disaster such as a flood, hurricane, or fire that damages your home. You call the insurance company and they mail you a three-page microscopically fonted document that describes in painful detail the steps you must take to file a claim. What do you do with the document?

A. Read each word with highlighter in hand.

B. Give the document to your spouse to read.

C. Call the insurance company and ask for a verbal explanation.

D. File the document in your homeowner's insurance policy file.

E. Throw the document in the garbage with a comment that you're sure someone will explain this to you if it is important.

Most of us are not motivated to learn unless there is a very specific, authentic use for the information. We don't read tax rules if we have a trusted accountant; we don't read the instruction manual for programming our cell phone if we have a teenager to program it for us; we don't read the "changes to your credit card" statement if we don't use that credit card— or even if we do. Students are not much different from the rest of us. If they are asked to read something that may apply to them at some future time or for which they can find no relevance, they most likely are not going to become engaged in the learning. We may create a purpose by testing them on the material, but soon after the test that information will be quickly relegated to a nonessential file in their brains. In fact, research exists that describes the "discrepancy between perceived and actual success" for learning (Brooks and Brooks 1999, 8). Perceived success is *performance*, such as a high grade on a test without the in-depth understanding or application of the learning for future endeavors.

Most parents can identify with this concept if they have looked for a used car with their teenager. You and your child experience intensive, collaborative learning as you memorize safety and mechanical ratings of dozens of cars and become experts on the ratio of engine size to gas mileage. Together, you learn how to look for recent oil changes, camouflaged bodywork, and slipping clutches. You also find that interest and insurance rates can vary depending upon the model and year of the car. It is important that the learning is valid and accurate. Your choice could have long-term consequences financially, as well as for your child's safety. For the period of time prior to the purchase, you become intent upon processing and retrieving car information accurately. After the purchase, the knowledge shifts to a mental file that may or may not be accessed again based upon need. The impetus for learning is based on a genuine purpose and the knowledge is meaningful to the learner. That's the nature of real learning and has been since the beginning of time.

Learning is directly related to its employment, that is, its relevance, purpose, and meaning as defined by the learner. Brain Cambourne describes this principle simply:

> In order to implement the principles of "use" most effectively in classrooms, teachers need to create settings in which learners experience an urgent need to read and write in order to achieve ends other than learning about reading and writing. Learners need time and opportunity to use, employ, and practice their development control in functional, realistic, and nonartificial ways. (1988, 74)

How can these "ways" be created in a classroom where the curriculum is preset and learning is mandated by standardized tests? For every lesson, think through the following questions to assess relevance or, better yet, ask students to complete a similar survey before beginning the topic of study as a way of helping them set a purpose for learning.

1. How is this lesson relevant to the lives of my students?
2. What is my pedagogical purpose in introducing students to this topic?
3. What meaning (outside of passing a test) will this unit have for my students?
4. How will this information help students in the future?
5. What background knowledge do students have that will increase understanding?
6. How can I help students connect prior knowledge with new learning?
7. How will assessment ensure that students' learning is for actual, not perceived, success?

Making Connections

> Man can learn nothing except by going from the known to the unknown.

—CLAUDE BERNARD

Making connections to prior or background knowledge is one of the most effective ways for students to retain and use learned information. It is a "Velcro" effect where new information attaches to what already exists. If there is not a matching Velcro piece, the chances of adhesion are very slim. Of course students must have a rich storehouse of background knowledge to make such sticky connections. But even students who have not had an educationally rich background have the capacity for connecting. Sometimes we have to help them probe for a connection—or we may have to help them create a connection. Serving up isolated information and hoping for absorption simply doesn't work. Saying that we have covered a topic sometimes means just that: the information covers students until they have the opportunity to crawl out from under. The way to avoid "covering" is by immersing them in the content and building background information so new knowledge is internalized and transformed into meaning.

Activate and build background knowledge by putting students in groups to share past experiences. Provide multiple resources as a way of creating layers of connections through supplemental texts, magazines, newspapers, audio books, videos, guest speakers, and field trips. In *I Read It but I Don't Get It,* Chris Tovani (2000) points out the importance of *text-to-text* connections, such as connecting new information to a book or movie; *text-to-self* connections, such as with a personal experience; and *text-to-world* connections, such as with a current event. If students come to class with a deficit of connections in the subject area, we have background work to do before we can begin to move forward with new learning. Following are suggested ways to help students build and activate background knowledge.

◆ Whenever possible, refer to events or scenes in movies or television shows that can be tied to the content area. For example, to help students connect to novels set during the depression, ask "How many of you saw the movie *Cinderella Man?* Do you remember when the mother added water to the milk? Why did she do that?"

◆ Have a designated student cut out the front page headlines each day and tape them to a poster under the date. Keep the headlines up as long as possible and refer to them at every opportunity to build and reinforce background knowledge.

◆ Ask students to share photographs or artifacts of experiences to personalize connection to the study. Students whose parents are in the military often have extensive collections of objects and photographs from countries around the world. A student who had visited Auschwitz while her father was stationed in Poland brought pictures and shared her experience, enriching the study of *The Diary of Anne Frank.*

◆ Brainstorming is an activity that reignites connections that students may not even realize they have. Before beginning a unit on a historical event, for example, have students list everything they know or think they know about the event. Cover chart paper or the boards with their notes, as well as lists from other classes. Have a student volunteer type up the final list and give a copy to each student. Have students circle phrases or words when there is some reference to them in the text.

◆ When studying a specific topic, check out books, magazines, and video-tapes from the library related to those topics. Give students an entire period or more to peruse, read, and discuss what they find in books and magazines. Provide a VCR for small groups to watch videos related to the topic.

Allowing students to share what they know and what they want to know before beginning a unit creates an intellectual environment of inquiry and engagement, but it is also essential to have a classroom that is rich with information and print. A subscription to a class set of magazines provides an opportunity for students to read and share in an authentic and purposeful way. In this era of differentiated instruction—better thought of as differentiated opportunities for individualized learning—communal magazine reading is a perfect way to have students access text at their own level of proficiency and interest. For almost ten years, while teaching a variety of high school courses such as English, law studies, debate, speech, economics, and U.S. government, I had a class subscription to *Time* magazine for my students. Each week students eagerly awaited the new issue because they had become familiar with features of the magazine: short takes, quotes, political cartoons, movie reviews, opinion pieces, and features on famous people. The thread of continuity, especially with letters to the editor about previous articles, created deep connections to topics that came alive for students. The class debates, discussions, projects, and writing that emerged from their reading were relevant and authentic, leading to deep insight and understanding.

For example, when racecar driver Dale Earnhardt was killed in a crash during a race and his picture was on the cover of *Time* magazine, the struggling readers in the class were immersed in the long article for days during independent reading time. I don't know the readability level of the text, but I do know these students were reading, discussing, and learning because they were engaged. Students have come back for years telling me that the best learning experience of their high school years was not what I taught them, but what I allowed them to learn by giving them access to *Time* magazine each week. Following are titles of current magazines that would be useful in content-area classes.

Time and *Newsweek*

◆ book and music reviews

◆ graphs, maps, charts, time lines

◆ in-depth features on current topics relating to science, social studies, politics, health, public figures, current events, art, movies

◆ photographs, illustrations

◆ medical section

◆ interviews

◆ essays and editorials

◆ numbers section, using fractions, percentages, ratios

◆ short takes on current popular culture issues and news items

Scientific American

◆ technology

◆ experiments

◆ new scientific theories

◆ electronics

◆ mechanics

◆ ask the experts

Why does inhaling helium make one's voice sound strange?

Why is fuel economy of a car better in summer than winter?

Popular Science

◆ what's new in technology

◆ car facts

◆ engineering

◆ how-to section

American Scientist

◆ biology (color photographs and labeled illustrations)

◆ sections on ecology, biology, physics, astronomy

◆ science observations

◆ biographies

◆ book reviews

◆ photographs and maps

◆ microscopic pictures and drawings

Dis\cover

◆ news about science, medicine, and technology

◆ short takes on science news

◆ biology

◆ in-depth special issues, such as one on Einstein

Psychology Today

◆ insights into the mind and behavior

◆ memories of the past

◆ relationships

◆ medicine

◆ new theories

Archaeology

◆ archaeological features and digs

◆ history

◆ interviews

◆ pictures of archaeological sites

American Artist

◆ quick sketches

◆ exhibitions

◆ methods and materials

◆ careers

◆ compositions

◆ features on artists

◆ hot markets: literary, mystery, automotive, aviation, military

◆ fiction writing (five ways to build better characters)

◆ author interviews (Louis Sachar, author of *Holes*)

Other Magazines Worth Exploring

Astronomy	*Poets and Writers*
Business 2.0	*Writer's Digest*
Civil War Times	*Writers' Journal*
American History	*Smart Money*
World War	*American Songwriter*
History	*Architectural Digest*

Staple student response sheets to the back of magazines or post them in the class as a way of having students share what they learned. (See Figure 7.1.)

Motivation for Using Learning: Using Prompts

> The teacher who is attempting to teach without inspiring the pupil with a desire to learn is hammering on cold iron.
>
> —HORACE MANN

When students research and share topics of interest to them, the environment becomes more like an active laboratory than a traditional classroom. Three days a week begin the class with a writing or discussion prompt presented by a student or small team. Each individual or group can be scheduled in advance and the assignment calendar prominently displayed. Model the process for the first several weeks of class, demonstrating appropriate and thought-provoking topics, such as those listed below.

Sample Writing and DiscussionPrompts

◆ *English:* Show a five-minute clip from the movie *Contact* where the main character takes a trip into space and experiences an epiphany regarding other life-forms. *Writing prompt:* What do you think the character experienced? Do you believe there is life beyond what we know on earth? Explain why you feel as you do.

Student Response Guide for Magazine Articles

Title of Magazine _____   Date of Issue _____

Title of Article(s) _____   Page Numbers _____

Author _____

1. Why did you choose this article to read?

2. What connections could you make from the article to what you have learned in this or other classes?

3. Was there anything in the article that you already knew?

4. List three new pieces of information or insights you gained from the article.

5. How will you use the information in the future?

6. In what way was the article interesting to you?

7. What other information do you wish the article would have included?

8. Was there anything in the article with which you did not agree? Explain.

9. List any new words that you learned from the article.

10. What will you do with this information? Choose one:

    a. letter to the editor

    b. discussion with classmate, parent, other

    c. response in learning log

    d. other _____

FIGURE 7.1

- *Social Studies/Law Studies:* Provide a news clip or newspaper article detailing the debate over Terri Schiavo, the young woman whose parents fought to keep her alive through an artificial feeding tube, although the courts ordered the tube be removed based on her husband's testimony. *Discussion prompt:* To what extent should the government intervene in the decisions of families to end the lives of those deemed vegetative? Who should make that decision?

- *Math:* Provide news articles or brochures related to hybrid cars and their gas mileage. *Prompt:* Compare the miles per gallon of a hybrid with your own car or your parents' car. What other advantages or disadvantages would come into play in purchasing such a car?

◆ *Science:* Provide an article from a science magazine about frogs with physical deformities due to chemical pollution in lakes and streams. *Writing prompt:* What other transformations in species might occur in your own area due to chemical pollution? What impact does this information have for humans in the future?

◆ *Psychology:* Demonstrate a popular video game. Ask students to note their heartrates, breathing, and mental process when watching the demonstration. *Writing prompts:* Do you believe there is any merit to the argument that video games can become addictive? As a parent, how would you monitor your child's video game use? Do players respond differently to different video games? Do you believe that playing violent video games can create violent behavior?

◆ *Generic:* Have the principal or superintendent visit the class and discuss a current issue, such as leaving campus for lunch, the attendance policy, or mandatory final exams. *Discussion prompts:* As a parent, how would you respond to the information? as a school board member? as a teacher? as a student?

Because such prompts are student-generated, the topics are relevant to students' lives and motivation is high. Students' writing improves with frequent use, and student leaders are often born as they facilitate discussions with their peers. Following is a sample format for a student discussion and writing prompt.

Prior to Prompt Day

Students should begin thinking about an appropriate topic several weeks prior to their assigned prompt day by doing one or more of the following:

◆ Watch news shows on television (such as *20/20, 60 Minutes,* or the local news). Videotape segments that might work as possible topics.

◆ Read newsmagazines (such as *Time* or *Newsweek*) or newspapers (such as the local paper or *USA Today*) for topics of interest.

◆ Interview someone who might be knowledgeable about a topic that interests them, such as a politician, professional, or teacher.

◆ Narrow their topics to specific, open-ended questions with no right or wrong answer, ones that will create deep thinking or generate various viewpoints of other students in the class.

At the Beginning of Prompt Day

Students should:

- Have some type of physical learning, such as those listed below, available to engage the class in the topic. It should last no longer than ten minutes.

  a clip of a videotape of a news show, movie, or television show

  a newspaper or magazine article

  an interview with someone knowledgeable on the topic

  a poem, short story, or opinion column

  a guest speaker who will speak for no longer than ten minutes

  an audiotape of a radio show (such as a segment on NPR) or a book on tape

- Present the background information to the class and write the prompt on the board or hand out copies of it. Decide in advance if the prompt will elicit a written or oral response.

- Remember to follow facilitator rules for discussion, such as

  one person speaks at a time

  engage students in discussion rather than stating your own views

  treat all speakers with respect

  probe for deeper thinking by asking thought-provoking questions

  continue to bring the discussion back to your prompt rather than allowing it to trail off in many directions.

Wrapping Up Prompt Day

Students should:

- Have some sort of conclusion: a quote, film snippet, or summary of the discussion. If students wrote in response to the prompt, ask volunteers to share their thoughts on the topic.

- Write a reflection of the experience, along with any notes or handouts, and give them to the teacher.

Often, prompts lead to more expansive projects. After a student prompt that generated a discussion on standardized testing, for example, a class organized a community forum, raising money to bring in a noted author on the topic. The evening included refreshments, a band, and much interest from the local media, who interviewed students and replayed parts of the event on the evening news. The entire event was supported by the school's administration and led to one of the student organizers obtaining an internship in her state representative's office.

In another instance, a high school English teacher was faced with the prospect of having her students complete a research paper. These struggling learners were often absent, and when they did attend they were disengaged, disinterested, and disruptive. When she told them it was time to do the required research paper, the students began thinking of ways to buy a completed paper or pay someone to do part of the work. Some students wanted to know if they could still pass if they failed the research paper part of the class. School had become a game with the teacher struggling to keep the pieces on the board. One day she closed the lid, put the board away, looked at her opponents and refused to play. She had decided that she was wasting everyone's time. Together, students and teacher brainstormed a way to make the assignment meaningful, something that would achieve more than moving a game piece on the board. Because interviewing was one part of the requirement, the class decided to interview residents of a nearby retirement home, write their stories, and compile them into a book that they would donate to the home. They found a way to conduct face-to-face interviews with residents by taking a school bus on field trips during the ninety-minute class. Residents of the home chose their student interviewers based on a questionnaire students filled out detailing their interests. Some students expressed an interest in historical events that may have taken place during the lifetimes of the residents; others listed hobbies or professions that residents may have had.

After the interview, students researched their topics to fill in the gaps, returned for a final interview, and finalized the project with quotes, photographs, and additional information. What occurred was a match of common interests and the mutual satisfaction that comes from relating to other human beings. This unusual research project also produced an unexpected respect that spanned generations and, in several cases, created enduring friendships.

In another example, a biology class began a composting project with the goal of selling the compost to the public. With the profits, the class wanted to build a greenhouse and use the compost to create soil that would sustain a variety of unusual plants that could be donated or sold the public.

During the initial phase of the project, a physical scientist with the environmental division of a local Air Force base heard of their project and arranged for three of the students from the class to accompany him on a trip to a composting conference in another state. At first, the conference organizers didn't know what to make of the request since students had never been a part of their seminar. They ended up waiving the fee for the students. In a "composting contest," held the last day of the conference, the three students and their scientist sponsor won second place. These students shared the videotape of their experience with the rest of the school and provided valuable tips that helped get the school's composting project on its feet.

Learning should be one of life's greatest pleasures, the most gratifying and fulfilling of experiences. The notion that greater benefits accrue for students when leaning is painful or difficult doesn't square with research or reality. As students encounter rich and complex learning experiences that are relevant to their own lives, they will discover the infinite joys of solving problems, finding patterns, and unraveling truths.

Using Learning with English Language Learners (ELL)

In *Meeting the Needs of Second Language Learners: An Educator's Guide*, Judith Lessow-Hurley advises, "Provide context for activities. Use visuals and hands-on activities whenever possible to help provide comprehensible language input" (2003, 79). What is *comprehensible language input?* It is what all students need to learn most effectively: purpose, relevance, meaning, and use for the activity. In the case of English Language Learners, that means using the language for a purpose other than to learn the language. As students become involved in a project where the skills and knowledge are relevant, the new language becomes an inherent and useful part of learning.

Using Learning: Study Groups for Teachers

Professional journals offer relevant and content-specific research, instructional practices, resources, and teaching tips. Short articles can be read in one setting and are less intimidating and time-consuming than tackling an entire book. Often journals stack up in professional libraries or on teachers' shelves because so many other pressing issues consume the day.

Using professional development time to read and share articles can be a valuable way to spark new ideas and infuse teachers with renewed energy.

Teacher Study Group: Reflection

Ask teachers to list the top three areas of interest in their teaching lives. A brainstorming session within content areas or in small groups during a faculty meeting will provide relevant reading material for the first session. Teachers may also wish to choose from a list, such as the one below. Spending time on this prereading activity will provide a purpose for the session, even if teachers change their minds once they begin to peruse the journals.

Journal Article Topics: Circle Three Topics of Interest to You

classroom management	response to student work
reading in the content area	use of data to guide instruction
writing in the content area	English Language Learners
vocabulary	supplemental texts
differentiated instruction	young adult novels in content areas
project-based learning	coaching
informal assessment	school leadership
adolescent development	content-specific topics

Teacher Study Group: Action

1. Collect professional journals from as many different sources as possible, such as from the district media center, the school's professional library, administrators, literacy coaches, and teachers. Display the journals in one place, grouping them according to topic, if possible. Be sure to include a wide variety of journals from all content areas and educational sources.

2. If time permits, have teachers read articles during the study group session, allowing up to forty-five minutes for reading. Provide sticky notes, pads of paper, pens, and highlighters. If possible, have a copier nearby so teachers can make their own copies of articles to save. If time is short, have teachers check out a journal and return for a separate discussion session.

3. Once the reading is finished, teachers may wish to complete the student response guide for magazines (see Figure 7.1, page 82) or revise the questions to fit their needs. A professional version of the response guide is shown in Figure 7.2.

Professional Article Response Guide

Title of Journal _____ Date _____

Title of Article _____

1. Write a response to what you read in the article.

2. What would you like to share with other teachers?

3. Is there anything in the article with which you disagree?

4. Choose one quote from the article that made an impact on you. Write it below.

5. How will you use the information in the article?

Group teachers according to topic of interest if possible and allow them to discuss the article, using this response sheet as a guide.

FIGURE 7.2

Teacher Study Group: Final Action Steps

Use the quotes that teachers copied from the article in one or more of the following ways:

1. Start a quote log that stays in the teachers' lounge so teachers can refer to quick bits of inspiration as a reminder of the value of professional journal reading.

2. Run off quotes and put them in teachers' boxes or use them on memos, newsletters, or official correspondence.

3. Post quotes on the bulletin board in the teachers' lounge.

4. Use quotes as discussion starters for study group sessions or to begin a faculty meeting.

Once teachers become aware of the value of professional journals, they will be hooked. Use professional development funds to order journal subscriptions and make the journals available to teachers as a powerful means of professional growth.

8

Learning by Approximation

Mistakes are, after all, the foundations of truth, and
if a man does not know what a thing is, it is at least
an increase in knowledge if he knows what it is not.

—CARL JUNG

Remember your first day of teaching? Your first week? That first long
year when you knew either that you would be a teacher forever or
you wondered what had ever possessed you to become a teacher
in the first place? List five mistakes you made in those early days. Beside
each, write what you learned from those mistakes. How do those lessons
compare to what you learned in college classes while obtaining your degree? What if you had been fired for making those mistakes?

I recently visited a teacher at the end of her first year who spent an
hour telling me all of the mistakes she had made in the classroom, how
much she had learned from her mistakes, and what she was going to try
next year based on her learning. She had been given the sponsorship of
the school yearbook, so her learning curve was not only steep, but her errors would be memorialized forever in a very large, hardbound book. The
fear of failure led her to do most of the "real" work for the yearbook her-
self, delegating to students less significant tasks such as sorting through
pictures instead of allowing them to write copy or lay out pages. "I cheated
students out of learning important skills," she mused. "Next year, from the
very beginning, they are going to be responsible for the yearbook. I am

going to expect more from them and teach them how to work together so they will have the pleasure of seeing the finished product of *their* work, not mine."

One of the most important elements in Brian Cambourne's theory of learning is the condition of approximation, where learners feel safe to approximate learning, that is, to take risks and make mistakes. Cambourne makes clear its importance: "Freedom to approximate is an essential ingredient of all successful learning" (1988, 70). He reminds us of how young children approximate as they begin to learn to talk. "Learner talkers are not expected to wait until they have all of the systems and sub-systems fully intact before they are allowed to talk. If this were the case they would not begin to produce audible speech until they were nine or ten years of age" (Cambourne 1995, 185). Furthermore, there is no anxiety associated with such early learning. In fact, every utterance, from a grunt to "mama," is met with warm approval, enthusiastic support, often loud applause. It is through this cycle of attempting the task, receiving feedback, and approximating learning that children begin the process of becoming fully functioning human beings; they learn to walk, speak, eat, and interact socially with others through a process of trial and error.

The condition of approximation is really an application of the scientific method. Cambourne reiterates, "When learning is looked at as a form of hypothesis testing, it becomes obvious that approximations (errors) are absolutely essential to the whole process" (1988, 67). It is, in fact, synonymous with the process of hypothesis, inquiry, and discovery: trying first one "educated guess," learning as much from the "guess" as from the success, and moving in total absorption to deeper learning. Without the freedom to inquire as a natural part of learning, the imposed ceiling may have long-lasting effects on learners' confidence in their intellectual abilities as well as on their ambition to try anything that does not come with an assurance of success.

Indeed, all learning thrives on the act of approximation. It is often only when children leave the secure nest of acceptance and encouragement and enter the arena of formal education that problems in learning occur. To subvert this process by failing to provide a safe environment where students can continue to experiment with learning is counterproductive and cruel. When learners are penalized for making mistakes by receiving low marks on a report card, being made to repeat a grade, or enduring any other form of humiliation, all bets for deep, intrinsic learning are off.

> Failure is instructive. The person who really thinks learns quite as much from his failures as from his successes.

— JOHN DEWEY

Help students become aware of learning by approximation by discussing it with them and providing opportunities for them to internalize its importance in their lives. First, have students form groups of three or four and choose a student facilitator who will lead the group in a discussion using the following guidelines:

◆ Read the first prompt to the group (see reflection prompts below). Allow a few minutes for quiet reflection.

◆ Ask one volunteer at a time to discuss his or her response. Other students must remain quiet until everyone has had a chance to respond to the prompt.

◆ After all members (including the facilitator) have had an opportunity to talk, allow five minutes for the group to discuss any thoughts they may have had while others were sharing.

◆ Move on to the next prompt, following the same procedure.

Reflection prompts may include:

1. Discuss mistakes you made as you learned something that is important to you, such as learning to play a sport or musical instrument.

2. What did you learn from your mistakes?

3. Think about a mistake that you made in school-related learning.

4. What was the result of the mistake?

5. Think of something that has been easy for you to learn. How do you learn best, such as through lab work, by reading, writing, listening to lectures, participating in an activity, watching someone who knows how to do what you want to learn, or watching video-taped instructions?

When the groups have finished discussing, ask volunteers to share with the entire class. Point out the importance of making mistakes as an essential part of learning. Have students return to their groups and create a graphic representation of learning, showing how approximation fits into the cycle. You may wish to share Cambourne's graphic cycle of his conditions for learning as a model (see Figure 2.1 on page 16). Post the students' illustrations on classroom walls to remind them of how natural learning occurs.

Unfortunately, we often seem to return to the tyranny of high-stakes testing and its direct conflict with Cambourne's conditions for learning, especially evident with the condition of approximation. Today, as I am writing this chapter, I glance at the front page of the *Atlanta Journal Constitution*. The headline reads, "Desperate schoolteachers: Under pressure for their students to perform well on national tests, some Georgia teachers break the rules." The article reports that much is "riding on the exams," such as student promotion, school reputations, and reassignment or firing of administrators and teachers. And what about the pressure on students who carry the weight of their teachers' futures with their "performance" on a single test? When there is no room for error, the space for learning also shrinks—sometimes to suffocating and frightening proportions.

Psychologically, when one's reality differs significantly from the reality he perceives is going on around him, the person may be in danger of entering an unstable mental state. Teachers and students may think they are in just such a state as they make remarkable progress in teaching and learning, but face a different reality in which the proof of such progress hinges on a single test. As Remonia Tooms, a fifth-grade teacher, said in the *Atlanta Journal* article (Donsky): "If your class is lucky enough to pass, then you are almost forbidden to fall below that level next year." Such a catch-22 is several levels beyond instability; it is insanity. Good teachers don't fall into the trap that is set by state and federal testing mandates. They know in the deepest parts of their teaching souls that human beings must make mistakes to learn, and that students who are held accountable to standards beyond their current reach often suffer emotional, psychological, and even physical illness.

For hundreds of generations, cultures have used trial and error as a means of learning for survival. History is full of examples of the value of making mistakes, and ironically, students are tested on their results by learning about people such as Thomas Edison, who experimented with thousands of different filaments to find just the right material to create the lightbulb's glow. Benjamin Franklin, Sir Isaac Newton, Alexander Graham Bell—to say nothing of modern-day scientists who are making errors right this minute in their quest for cures to debilitating diseases—understood the concept of approximation, mistakes that are a vital part of significant achievement. Modern schooling, with its percentiles and grade point averages, its rubrics and bell curves, its adequate yearly progress and standardized testing, has failed to learn from the lessons of the past. As Teddy Roosevelt reminded Americans were who struggling in another difficult time, "There is no effort without error or shortcoming." If our goal is for students to live the platitudes found on posters in most U.S. schools, if we want them to soar above the ordinary, to reach for the stars, to be all they can be—we must not insist that they get it right every time they try.

Cambourne notes that the condition of approximation is one that teachers understand but find difficult to implement in the classroom (1988, 66). Math and science teachers generally are more comfortable with the concept because they see the evidence of learning in false starts and the necessity of probing as a way of understanding. In the past, English teachers have been accused of "bleeding" on students' papers as they redmarked grammatical errors and spelling mistakes. It is possible that this act helped create the phenomenon of writer's block, that common condition that puts writers in a mind vacuum, unable to eke out a flowing sentence, sometimes even a few words, for fear of committing to paper a mistake. Once students become accustomed to writing rough drafts, revising their drafts, and editing with peers, the pressure decreases and the process of learning becomes as important as the product. Students are then able to develop the confidence to overcome the freeze of failure.

Encourage students to try various ways of reaching learning goals, and reassure them that not only is it okay, but it is also *necessary* to make mistakes as an important part of learning. Give them permission to fail.

One of the best ways to help students approximate is by having them employ higher thinking skills as they analyze their own work. Once students realize that most learning is "in process" rather than finished, they will accept the concept of approximation as a natural learning occurrence. Of course, grades discourage the act of approximating, but since most teachers have no choice but to assign a score so it can be translated to a report card grade, consider responding to students' work at every stage until students feel comfortable enough to submit it for a final grade. Show them how to analyze their own work and learn from their mistakes instead of relying on someone else to point out or fix their errors. Encourage students to revel in their own learning.

Once an assignment, paper, or project is graded, allow students the option of resubmitting the assignment for additional credit. The following is an example of a resubmission form, which may be tailored as needed for students' assignments.

Student Resubmission Form for Projects and Written Assignments

1. Describe how you completed the assignment (time, effort, difficulties).

2. Which part of the assignment would you like to redo? Why?

3. Have you had a conference with the teacher? Did she respond to the assignment in a written form? What did you learn from her comments?

4. Did another teacher, student, or a parent respond to the assignment? What did you learn from their comments?

5. What is your goal in revising this assignment?

6. What did you learn about yourself as you worked on this assignment?

7. What did you learn about the subject as you worked on this assignment?

8. What part of the process did you find most enjoyable or fulfilling?

9. What will you do differently with future assignments or tasks similar to this one?

10. Are you ready to submit this assignment for a final grade?

While tests can be useful assessment tools to determine students' strengths and needs for future instruction, students have been programmed to equate test grades with knowledge, dismissing future learning as "too late to matter" since the grade is already in the grade book. As a result, instructive teacher comments are often not read, sometimes thrown away, or placed in a notebook never to be looked at again. The testing system in U.S. schools has not encouraged the notion of testing as a learning tool. While the following form—which students submit along with each test that he or she wants to have reconsidered—may increase the workload for the teacher initially, the long-range benefits will be immense, and students will begin to make fewer errors on tests because they are learning to analyze their responses within the context of their own learning. The entire concept of testing can change as students begin to understand that true learning, an ongoing process, belongs to them alone.

Student Resubmission Form for Tests

1. Highlight the test items that you would like to resubmit on the original test and return it with this form attached.

2. Why did you answer the question as you did?

3. How did you come to learn the correct answer? (Or, if you believe your original answer is correct, defend it.)

4. Explain in detail how your understanding about the answer to this question has changed. Include any resources (such as teachers, parents, other students, books, internet, and so on) that aided your understanding.

Since grades are an entrenched part of schooling, the teacher must address how she will "award points" for resubmitted test items and specify deadlines. An advantage of using this form may be the elimination of unpleasant exchanges with students about the "correctness" of their answers when tests are returned, as well as a decrease in the flurry of makeup work that often appears on the teacher's desk minutes before grades are due.

Learning Again

> Everyone should learn to do one thing supremely well because he likes it, and one things supremely well because he detests it.

> —B. W. M. Young

Cambourne refers to approximation—attempting to emulate a demonstration—as "having a go" (1988, 69). At the end of your course, allow students the joyful freedom of having a go at learning. Students must choose to learn something that they found difficult in your course, such as the concept of the bull and bear markets in economics, electrical energy in science, T. S. Eliot in English, or theorems in math. Since this exercise will come at the end of the course, have students think of one part of the course they were most relieved to have finished, a topic that was difficult or uncomfortable for them to learn. Allow them to experiment with learning in a stress-free environment where every step of the learning is encouraged and celebrated. The activity is all about fostering intrinsic motivation, so this final learning project should not be graded beyond a completion mark.

Having a Go at Learning

1. Spend at least one class period in which you and the students review the curriculum of the course. In groups or as a whole class, have students jot down topics they found easy to learn and topics they had

difficulty with or may not have learned at all. Remind them that test scores or grades may not indicate authentic learning. These written reflections will be a valuable assessment of students' learning as a whole and can be used as data to drive instruction with future classes.

2. Students should then choose one topic they want to relearn. Have students answer the following questions before beginning the project.

   ◆ Which topic will you "have a go" at learning?

   ◆ Describe how you will learn the material.

   ◆ What resources outside of class will you use?

3. If possible, pair each student with a classmate who will serve as a mentor during the learning process. It would be preferable, but not necessary, for the mentor to have a good foundation in the material to be learned.

4. On the due date, students may share what they learned with the class. Encourage a variety of products, such as an oral presentation, a written paper, media presentation, or artistic representation.

A culture that encourages learning in an environment where one is free to take intellectual risks cannot survive in a vacuum. It must happen in a place where approximation is the order of the day. A school must seek a change in the intellectual climate, in the attitudes of students, teachers, administration, support staff—literally everyone associated with the school. There must be a firm commitment to learning, not testing, as the highest goal, and such a philosophy must be reflected in every action played out on the daily stage of schooling. In short, the entire school community must understand and value approximation as an essential ingredient for all learning and nothing should compromise its existence.

Learning by Approximation with English Language Learners (ELL)

The condition of approximation is especially important for English Language Learners. Without the opportunity to "have a go" at their new language in an atmosphere where they are free to take risks with unconditional support, their new learning will freeze in place and they will retreat to the safety of their own language. Not surprisingly, many studies of students learning a new language reveal the importance of having them move at their own rate, *attempt* the verbal reproduction of the new language, and learn in a nonstressful environment.

Learning by Approximation: Study Groups for Teachers

Teacher Study Group: Reflection

Provide the following two quotes from Cambourne and ask study group members to respond to them:

> Without the opportunity to approximate, the whole, smooth-running learning cycle is stopped and progress and/or refinement becomes impossible. (1988, 69)

> Approximation is one of the conditions of natural learning which teachers find easiest to understand but most difficult to implement. (1988, 66)

Use the following discussion guide to form a connection between the concept of approximation and common experiences in the classroom.

1. Brainstorm mistakes you have made as a teacher/administrator.
2. What did you learn from your mistakes?
3. List mistakes that you have seen students make as they are learning.
4. What did they learn from their mistakes?
5. What is this school's attitude toward mistakes?
6. How can this school utilize mistakes as a way to help students learn?

Teacher Study Group: Action

Each study group member will choose one teaching practice that, for some reason (fear, lack of time, resources, or support) was unsuccessfully implemented. Consider the following options:

◆ something you tried in the past that was not successful
◆ something you wanted to try but were afraid would have negative results
◆ something your students wanted to try as a part of their learning, but you felt uncomfortable implementing

◆ something you learned about at a conference, through a journal article, or from another teacher, but did not feel "safe" enough to try yourself

Members should then form pairs or triads and share the instructional practice they will implement during the next few weeks. Note that each teacher may well have a different instructional practice that he or she wants to try in the classroom. The purpose of pairing is to provide a coach for each person to support these endeavors. Give time for the groups to discuss their plans, using the following questions as a guide:

1. Tell your idea to your coach.

2. When will you try this new practice?

3. In what ways can your coach support you?

   ◆ observing the lesson and providing objective notes

   ◆ coteaching with you

   ◆ discussing the logistics of the lesson prior to trying it in class

   ◆ analyzing the lesson with you afterward

   ◆ helping you obtain supplies and/or resources for the lesson

   ◆ listening actively as you talk through the process before, during and after its implementation

Teacher Study Group: Final Action Steps

Begin the meeting by showing members the two Cambourne quotes they discussed at the previous meeting. Ask if their perspective has changed based on their experiences. Allow time for each member to share his or her experience.

1. Describe what you tried in your classroom and how your students responded to the lesson.

2. Describe how having a "coach" altered the experience.

3. Allow the coach to comment as necessary.

As faculty members learn to rely on each other for encouragement, support, and professional advice, they will become more willing to try things that they may have been reluctant to experiment with in the past. More importantly, the very culture of the school will change as staff members approximate through trials, errors, and successes.

9

Learning Through Response

Ms. Marcus
says
line breaks help
us figure out
what matters
to the poet
don't jumble your ideas
Ms. Marcus says
every line
should count.

—JACQUELINE WOODSON, *LOCOMOTION*

W hen I was going through my tumultuous teenage years, uncon-
sciously following the conditions of learning to take on the man-
tle of adulthood, I experienced one of the most poignant responses of my life, one that would become a part of me and alter who I was
to become. I suspect most of us have had such an experience; someone responded to your actions in such a way that it inspired you, changed your
course, or shut you down—in any case inalterably affecting your life.

I was not a perfect teenager. I did the things most kids of that age do,
making my parents worry about my future and my ability to make wise decisions. I remember one particular night when my parents and I were argu-
ing about my choice of friends and activities. I was most likely defensive
and contrary, but I can still hear my father's words: "We don't agree with
you, but we always will be on your side, no matter what." Here were people
with whom I was furious, people I perceived were trying to control my life,

telling me they were on my side—and I knew they were. Such feedback to my actions, my learning, was transformational.

In later years, I found myself repeating the same words to my students and then to my own children. My father's response had replicated itself through me to future generations and their reaction was similar to mine: they softened, listened, and learned that it was possible to disagree with people, even disappoint them, and they still would remain your staunch ally.

Response is a powerful force; it can be a stimulating motivator or a suffocating inhibitor. Recall someone's response to your own learning that stands out as significant, either negatively or positively. Think of a time that you responded to students' learning in such a way that it made an obvious impact on them. What factors set that particular response apart from the hundreds of thousands of other responses you uttered to students in your classes?

Learning as We Go

It is best to learn as we go, not go as we have learned.

—Leslie Jeanne Sahler

Learning, according to Brian Cambourne, must include the condition of response: feedback from exchanges with more knowledgeable others. He clarifies the concept of response by saying, "While exchanges may vary in detail and richness . . . they have certain things in common: a) they are readily available, frequently given, nonthreatening and *with no strings attached*; b) there is no penalty for not getting the conventional form correct the next time it is produced. There is no limit to the number of exchanges that are offered and given" (Cambourne 1988, 40).

We wouldn't recognize Cambourne's definition of response in many of our country's secondary schools. Study sheets are passed out as if knowledge exists only at the end of question marks; tests are created, given, evaluated, and assigned a grade by a teacher; the average grade for a semester is calculated by a computer program that is failsafe; and the final GPA is adjusted. If it is too low, students will not play sports or go on to the next grade; if it is high enough, extrinsic awards will be offered as a tangible response for exemplary learning.

Consider, also, the many commercial programs that rely on electronic diagnostic tests to determine students' reading grade level, despite tremendous variations in the text's subject matter or the student's background knowledge and interest. Once a grade level has been assigned, often without the examiner speaking directly to the students, they are allowed to choose books only on their predetermined level. Students' responses to the reading take the form of still another test. The answers are scored as correct or incorrect and if a passing grade is obtained, the student can add that book to his competitive bean count—with the ultimate goal of winning a prize. Often, there is little, if any, meaningful discussion about the content of the book or about the range of human emotions that good literature evokes and confirms. Students need opportunities to choose books they want to read and broaden that experience by communicating with others. They need feedback that has the potential to expand their understanding and deepen their insights. It is the way humans learn. Until the concept of *response* is altered to reflect Cambourne's research, we will continue to misuse this most valuable learning tool and deny its benefits to students.

Teacher Response Analysis Guide

What is your response quotient? Use the following guide to help you reflect on the type of feedback you provide to students.

1. Do you respond to students in authentic ways as a natural part of conversation?

2. Do students ask you to respond to their work informally, such as through email or after school?

3. Do you withhold responses until the end of the unit?

4. Are your responses typically quantitative, such as through rubrics, or qualitative, such as in the form of oral or written comments?

5. Do you print out grades or post test scores as responses?

6. Do students often appear nervous or anxious about asking for your response?

7. Do students react positively, both verbally and with their body language, when you respond to them?

8. What, if any, strings are attached to your responses?

9. How do you define a "correct answer"?

10. How many chances are students given to find an answer?

11. Do you withhold responding to a student because you don't want to appear to be giving unfair advantage to one student over another?

12. Do you prefer giving one type of feedback over another (face-to-face, in writing, graphically, through analogies, a numerical score)?

The questions on this survey may be difficult to answer because they address the facets of individual personalities. A warm, affable person who genuinely enjoys conversations and delights in being around adolescents may find it easier to create a classroom where frequent, meaningful responses are a natural way of learning. Those who may be more reluctant to open up, share personal experiences, or respond in informal ways may revert to the safety of numerical grades as responses. Often, a particularly challenging class of students may make spontaneous responses difficult or impossible. At any rate, quality feedback depends upon a wide variety of factors, such as the disposition of students, the type of learning, and, perhaps ultimately, the personality of the teacher. The goal is to incorporate as many authentic, meaningful responses into the learning environment as possible and move away from responding to students only with the carrots and clubs of grades.

Learning to Respond

The authority of those who teach is often an obstacle to those who want to learn.

—Cicero

Responding Versus Assessing

For those who find it difficult to respond more openly, consider the following prompts as a way of developing an eventual ease with this process and as a starting point for responding rather than evaluating student work.

1. Why did you choose to . . . (work the problem in such a way, read that particular book, include this topic in your project)?

2. How might your thinking have changed if you had . . . ?

3. I was wondering . . .

4. Have you considered . . . ?

5. Your approach to this assignment is different than I expected. I have some questions:

6. I'm not sure I understand. Will you explain . . .

7. I had an experience similar to the one you are describing. What happened was . . .

8. This is a difficult concept to learn. Sometimes doing this will help . . .

9. Look again at what you wrote here. It's still not clear to me. Could you add details, or examples?

10. You have a unique angle to this project. I think you ought to pursue this and consider submitting it (for publication, in the science fair).

11. You have some interesting insights, but your (organization, grammar, sentence structure) will distract the reader from your ideas. Let's see how I (or a reference book, another student, internet site) can help you with that.

12. I want to know more. What else happened?

13. How does this part of your project relate to your thesis (or goal, purpose)?

14. There's something happening in your paper that I can't quite put my finger on. Do you feel comfortable asking _____ to read and respond to it?

15. This part of the assignment is so well thought out—it's brilliant! Toward the end, however, you seemed to lose some of your momentum. Can you figure out why?

In other words, respond to students' attempts at learning as you might to your own child who is having difficulty with homework, a spouse who needs your advice on a project, a peer who asks what you think about a teaching practice. You should give the student an honest response—not as an expert, but as a fellow human being who is there to help.

Although rubrics have become increasingly popular for almost every assignment in every course, rubrics by their very nature stifle authentic response. They provide a nice, neat format for arriving at a numerical grade, but in so doing, they often limit students' initiatives for creativity and deep learning outside the parameters of the assignment. Assigning points to "parts" of learning diminishes having students take responsibility for "how, why, and what" they will learn and firmly places the "more knowledgeable other" as an evaluator. Beware of rubrics that inadvertently become instruments that quash the apprentice concept that is so crucial to long-term learning.

Responding as a Colearner

> Students recognize when a teacher has passion for his or her field, is eager to lean new things, and brings genuine questions into the classroom for them to explore as partners.
>
> —KATHLEEN CUSHMAN, *FIRES IN THE BATHROOM*

Teachers who see themselves as a colearners are often those who seem to have an intuitive gift for teaching. Their characteristics are varied, but the one quality that seems consistent is that they actively listen because they want to understand, and they ask questions because they want to know. It is a different way of perceiving teaching, moving from the "sage on stage" model to a circle of dialogue and feedback based on a reciprocal need not only to understand what the other person is saying but also to *know* that person. It comes from caring about people as humans, not numbers, and valuing the eternal cycle that forms the most essential of human interactions: *conversation.*

Help students learn the difference between a response and an assessment as they form a synergistic network in the classroom, taking the burden off the teacher as the only knowledgeable one. Show students how to rely on each other's strengths and elicit authentic responses from each other in their continuing quest to learn. As students learn how to ask for feedback, the responsibility for their learning will return to them and they will seek the specific feedback *they* need, not what someone else thinks they may need or what the curriculum guide says they need. Imagine putting together a swing set with what seems like a million large and small pieces and hundreds of drawings and directions. Think of your relief when someone who has experience in swing set construction arrives to offer advice and demonstrate some of the most difficult parts of the procedure. Your chances for learning will be greater and less stressful as you ask questions and receive feedback from your friend. You will know you are successful when you see the final product that looks like the picture on the box. No rubric needed; no grade required.

As students learn, specifically when they are reading to learn, whether a textbook, math problem, novel, poem, essay, political cartoon, or countless other forms of writing, they will be more successful if they are able to have close contact with what Louise Rosenblatt refers to as "a mind uttering its sense of life" (1976). That's why it works so well to have high school students act as big brothers or sisters—mentors—to elementary students, especially as they are learning to read, or to pair a freshman who feels uncomfortable with the writing process with a senior who plans to major in journalism in college. One-on-one feedback from those who have been there is worth more than all the packaged programs, brightly colored textbooks, or educational gimmicks in the entire school.

Responding to Each Other

Place students in pairs and keep a wide variety of response sheets in places that are easily accessible to students. You may wish to provide specific prompts related to the text for some assignments and more general prompts for other types of reading, but students should know that they can find suggestions to prompt their thinking—to keep them from "getting stuck"—in a certain place, much like the Help option on their computers. Ask students to read silently for a specified period of time and then use a feedback guide (see below) to elicit responses from their partner. Hopefully, the guide will not be needed as the year progresses and students learn how to respond meaningfully to each other without the use of prompts. The teacher should engage with students during this process, providing feedback and scaffolding learning as needed.

Sample Prompts to Elicit Feedback

1. What questions did you have as you were reading?

2. Were there words you didn't know and couldn't figure out?

3. Were there words you knew, but they were used in a different way?

4. Does the material make sense to you? If not, in what way is it confusing?

5. What do you wish had been in the text that wasn't there?

6. If you had to report on this information to the media, what would you emphasize?

7. If you could gain further information on this topic, what would you want to know?

8. How would you present the material to make it clearer to classmates? What props, resources, visual aides, and so on, would you use?

9. What background knowledge did you bring to the topic?

10. What did you visualize as you read this text?

11. Would you like to reread any part of the text aloud to help with your comprehension of the text? Or would you like to listen as I read it?

12. What part, if any, appealed to you? Why?

13. How does this relate to what you learned earlier or in another class?

14. If you could have a conversation with the author about the text, what would you ask or say?

15. How might this text be portrayed in a movie?

Partners may not have answers to the questions, of course, but the authentic dialogue and interaction will lead to a more critical analysis of the reading, allowing students time and space to reflect with another learner. Whole class discussions with teacher feedback should follow small group sessions.

Responses from those other than classmates and the teacher are also powerful motivators to learners. Coaches and athletes understand this concept very well, and have taken positive feedback to new heights with pep rallies, cheerleaders, spirit sections, and banner-waving rows of loyal fans. They know that such support and immediate feedback will encourage athletes to perform at their optimal levels, maybe even to set new records. This same model will work for academic learners. Students are never too old to bask in admiration from their parents or friends. Create "shows" of learning and invite students and parents for an in-class or evening performance. Events such as debates, role-playing, history fairs, math team competition, art shows, and poetry readings garner positive feedback and provide an authentic purpose for learning.

Perhaps the most important type of feedback is generated from within the students themselves. In our quest to create independent learners, we should help students learn how to evaluate their own learning. This is the process-not-product mentality that will allow students to be critically aware of their own thinking along the way. Eventually, the above prompts should become internalized by students as they analyze their own reading, writing, thinking, and hypothesizing. They should question constantly, taking on the role of "the more knowledgeable other" for themselves. Students who lose the efficacy or confidence to look at their own work and, instead, turn it over for evaluation by someone else are not growing in independence or acquiring the vital skills they will need to enter adulthood as productive decision makers. One of the most important skills that teachers can help students develop is the ability to respond honestly to their own learning.

Student Prompts for Self-Evaluation

1. Does the assignment accomplish what I intended? If not, what more do I need to do?

2. If I look at my work from another angle, perhaps taking an opposing position, have I adequately addressed all points?

3. Have I let the assignment "cool" so that I can read it with new eyes and see any glaring mistakes or inconsistencies?

4. Could I delve into this topic in a deeper manner, one that will make the reader or listener think in new and different ways?

5. Am I satisfied with my work? Does it reflect my own ideas and new learning?

6. Which part of my work could be improved?

7. Which part of my work am I most satisfied with?

8. Have I looked at the smallest details to see if I have overlooked anything or misinterpreted facts?

9. If I had to evaluate my work in one sentence, what would it be?

10. How is this assignment meaningful or relevant to my learning?

Engineers, doctors, lawyers, architects, scientists, mechanics, musicians, artists, writers, and actors, to name a few, have turned their learning into professions, and they continue to learn through daily experience and frequent, authentic feedback. If they ignore feedback from others and are incapable of self-evaluation, they may not have a profession, or at least a successful one. Such a concept is obvious, a truism that everyone accepts without argument. Why, then, is it considered so beyond the pale, out of the box, even subversive in some districts and states to demand that responses to students' work be, according to Cambourne, "readily available, frequently given, nonthreatening, with no strings attached, and not carrying a penalty for not getting the conventional form correct the next time it is produced" (1988, 187)? To do less is to set our students up for frustration and failure in place of the success they so richly deserve.

Learning Through Response with English Language Learners (ELL)

When very young children begin to learn language, they test their knowledge by gauging the feedback of others. If they point to a cup and say "cat," the caregiver responds by asking, "Do you mean you want a CUP?" She may give the cup to the child and repeat "CUP" or point to the cat and say clearly, "CAT." The feedback is relevant, timely, authentic, and there is no penalty for the error. When English Language Learners try out a new language, sometimes at a similarly simple level, the feedback should be equally straightforward, with no strings attached. It is by paying attention to the responses of others that the ELL student learns the most valuable lessons of all.

Learning Through Response: Study Groups for Teachers

In secondary schools, where isolation can be a problem, teachers tend to form relationships with those in the same department or team, or with teachers who have common planning periods. Even so, there is little time for social conversations, much less for professional dialogue. Despite the overwhelming research that clearly demonstrates how positive change occurs in schools where there are opportunities for collaboration among teachers, most schools cut such opportunities short. Collaboration, like any quality relationship, requires time to talk, address common challenges, and form bonds of trust with each other.

Teacher Study Group: Reflection

Begin the session by asking members to spend at least ten minutes freewriting about the most enjoyable and rewarding aspects of their school day. They should then spend ten minutes writing as a way of purging—using this time to unload the many difficulties or pressing challenges they may face in any given school day.

Teacher Study Group: Action

Ask members individually to list five challenges and five positive aspects of their teaching lives on index cards.

Create two charts: *challenges* and *rewards*. Go around the group and have each member list one challenge and one reward. Continue the process until everyone has given all of his or her listed challenges and rewards. If someone repeats what has already been noted, place a checkmark beside the original item. Ask members to choose one item from the rewards chart that they would like to discuss. Put members in small groups according to similar topics. Allow at least fifteen minutes for groups to dialogue about the topic. Sample conversation starters include:

◆ Did you expect this reward when you first became a teacher?

◆ In what way does this reward affect your students' learning?

◆ What are other aspects of this reward that you may not have thought about?

◆ How often do you experience the benefits of this reward?

◆ How does this reward compare to other rewards in your personal life?

Then have members choose one item from the challenge list and form small groups based on similar challenges. Allow another fifteen minutes for conversation. Sample conversation starters include:

◆ In what ways does this challenge affect your ability to teach your students?

◆ Is this challenge something over which you have control? If not, can you let it go?

◆ If so, what steps can you take to overcome the challenge?

◆ Who do you need to contact for help with this challenge? How will you solicit help from this person?

◆ Are there ways around this challenge that you may not have considered?

Give 5-10 minutes at the end of the session for members to record any reflections, thoughts, or ideas they gained from the conversations.

Teacher Study Group: Final Action Steps

Members should keep a journal until the next meeting, recording specific times and places that the rewards manifested themselves, such as with a specific student or during a particular class. They should also keep notes that relate to the challenges, writing briefly any new ideas or perspectives that address the challenge, as well as any attempts to resolve or overcome the difficulty. At the next meeting, members should get into their original rewards and challenges groups and continue the dialogue, hopefully bringing new insights as a result of the collaboration.

Asking questions, seeking feedback, readjusting beliefs, and engaging in new practices will weave a tight fabric of learning that will wrap beautifully around the shoulders of even our most reluctant learners.

Section Two

Engagement Through Learning Communities

Who dares to teach must never cease to learn.

—JOSEPH JOUBERT

For years teachers have dreaded inservice training. I remember being called from my room to attend a presentation on a valuable half-day when students were released early. My team teacher and I were trying to hide out, hoping our absence would not be noticed as we planned a project we wanted to introduce to students the next day. Students were reading about the 1960s in a special edition of *Time* magazine, and we were planning to have them interview someone who lived through a significant event of the 1960s. Just as the creative juices began flowing, we were startled by the assistant principal who had been sent to find us. He said the principal wanted *everyone* to hear the afternoon's speaker. Feeling like caught fugitives, we made our way to the cafeteria and spent the afternoon listening to a well-intentioned presenter showing us plastic gadgets and clever tricks that she promised would engage students in high school curriculum. As I recall, during the presentation we wrote furtive notes to each other about our 1960s project, feeling at once childish and indignant at being treated as if we didn't know how best to spend time that would benefit our students.

111

In the past several years, research has turned sit-and-get professional development on its head. With powerful findings by such researchers as Bruce Joyce and Beverly Showers (2002), we now know that no matter how excellent the information or how knowledgeable, motivating, or engaging the presenter, without support from peers in the form of some type of collaboration, the learning teachers gain from isolated professional development has little transfer to the classroom. Even inservice that clearly defines the area of study, demonstrates instructional techniques, and provides opportunities for teachers to practice the new skills doesn't necessarily benefit students. In fact, only about 5 percent of the participants will transfer their training to the classroom, even under the best of circumstances. When the key element of peer coaching or collaborative support is added, that percentage rises to an amazing 95 percent (Joyce and Showers 2002, 79). Clearly, my students would have benefited much more if my colleague and I had spent time planning for their learning instead of being ushered to the cafeteria for a presentation that was not relevant to our curriculum or to the students' needs.

Why the sudden shift to professional development in a book about engaging adolescents? The engagement of teachers has everything to do with the engagement of students. Disengaged teachers cannot hope to engage their students, and teachers who spend class periods teaching isolated material that has little relevance to students or orchestrating test prep exercises are acting much like the one-shot professional developer whose presentation may look good on the outside but makes little impact on students' learning.

In addition, teachers who function alone outside of a community struggle to remain engaged. Schools are a collective endeavor, yet too often teachers are solitary in their work, isolated from a supportive network, working alone in a profession fraught with complex and ever-changing challenges. Walking into a classroom sometimes reminds me of a scene from *Star Wars* where the spaceship is speeding through a vast darkness with blinding shooting lights, zinging, pinging fragments of noise, and near-collisions with unrecognizable bodies. While there is much to be said for the excitement of a classroom environment, it is often a destabilizing and disorienting journey when the teacher tries to take command of the ship. Teachers, as well as students, deserve support—a secure home base where they can connect to other travelers.

Thus, words such as *collaboration, professional learning teams, peer coaching,* and *leadership teams* have come to replace traditional inservice offerings where days are carved out of the school calendar months in advance and topics that have little, if anything, to do with what is going on in the classroom are set in stone on a generic agenda. Thomas Guskey, in *Evaluating Professional Development*, defines professional development as a *process* that is intentional, ongoing, and systemic (2000, 16). Carol Lyons and Gay Pinnell, in *Systems for Change in Literary Education*, talk about process as "the ways people engage in learning so that they build commitment and ownership, form a community with shared meanings. Process provides for continuous learning about content" (2001, 184). Laura Robb, in *Redefining Staff Development*, offers a model of professional study where she views "schools as centers of inquiry, where teachers and administrators pose questions, pinpoint problems, study, reflect, and collaborate to discover possible answers. [Staff development] is both dynamic and flexible, responding to and integrating into the study process the diverse needs of faculty and administrators" (2000, 19). All of this sounds quite a bit like the process of learning itself.

Actually, the new and improved professional development fits Brian Cambourne's model of learning very well. In reviewing the conditions that must be in place for learning to occur, consider its relationship to staff development.

Teachers who are immersed in a topic of study or inquiry, not for the purpose of putting in time for inservice credit but in an ongoing process of discovery, create a powerful culture of learning. Schools that house up-to-date professional libraries with books and journals that address a variety of pedagogical issues and provide the necessary time for teachers to engage in active study based on their students' needs are immersing the staff in a type of professional development that has far-reaching benefits. Even those who are reluctant to take part in such staff development gain something from the daily association with a learning community. Conversely, when faculty meetings focus more time on housekeeping items than on dialogue that reaches to the heart of learning, true reform is truncated. These schools may run like clockwork, but at the end of the year, students and teachers wonder what they have done with their time.

Schools of learning are places where professional jealousy does not exist because the environment simply will not cultivate it; instead teachers spend planning time observing peers from whom they might gain a bit of understanding. It is a place where one leans on the strength of another and learns from those strengths by watching peers in action.

Professional development in all its forms, from reading and English Language Learner endorsements to a set number of inservice hours necessary for recertification, has often been a hoop-jumping exercise tangentially related to classroom application. Currently, despite research embracing systemic staff development and collaborative support, teachers feel increased pressure of performance goals that swirl ominously around high test scores. Such an overt message to teachers about their worth and the importance of their profession can only lead to discouragement and disengagement.

Fortunately, teachers are masters of flexibility. They know that what works beautifully in one class can turn out to be a total disaster in another. Because teachers facilitate learning with students who possess a wide variety of skills, background knowledge, and interests, it is difficult, if not impossible, to predict what will work. That is why approximation may be one of the most important learning conditions for teachers. In order for learning to occur, mistakes are essential. Teachers must feel secure enough to try something new, evaluate its effectiveness, and try again. Learning from making mistakes is what creates exemplary teachers; those who refuse to wander outside the confines of their own teaching parameters (or those imposed upon them) will rarely rise above mediocrity. Teaching is an art that is constantly forming and reforming itself based on an infinite mix of factors that often change moment to moment. In schools that encourage change as a result of new learning, the culture must cushion teachers as they find the courage and tenacity to break out of the familiar.

Differentiated instruction is an example of "new" learning that drives many teachers to distraction. "What is it?" some ask, and then discover that innovative teachers who teach to the strengths and needs of individual students have been differentiating instruction for years. When teachers attend workshops on differentiated instruction, they quickly learn its definition and can provide many examples of differentiating the content, process, or product of their curriculum. Putting such a theory into action is an entirely different thing, however. Perhaps more than any other practice, the success of differentiated instruction relies on practice and approximation—trying out instruction in a variety of ways and with various groups of students. Because it isn't something that can be mastered, differentiated instruction requires ongoing approximation to create a comfort level with the process.

Much of the responsibility that teachers once assumed for their own learning has been commandeered by local, state, and federal governments. With standards, benchmarks, and razor-sharp accountability, teachers, in truth, often don't have the privilege of using new learning in their practice. Ironically, while professional development research confirms that ownership is a key element in effective staff development, the pressure put on teachers to conform to a preset curriculum—which often includes teaching only what will be tested—forces them to answer to test makers rather than to their best professional judgment and internal, creative muse. The power in taking responsibility, then, must come from a collaborative effort. Leadership teams, literacy councils, peer coaches, and study groups must assume ownership of their learning and enjoy the freedom to demonstrate, practice, and use what they have learned. Learning, even life-altering learning, will remain in a vacuum, powerless and barren, until engagement with authentic, meaningful use brings it to life.

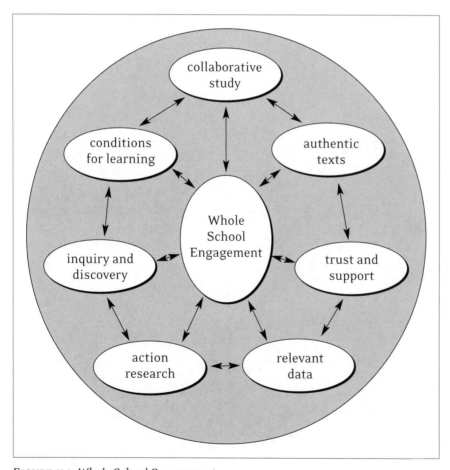

FIGURE II.1 *Whole School Engagement*

10

Engagement Through Study Groups

The illiterate of the twenty-first century will not be those who cannot read and write, but those who cannot learn, unlearn, and relearn.

—ALVIN TOFFLER

Imagine a school where engagement is at the center of all learning; consider teachers and students involved in activities where teams of learners are supported as they discover, reflect, and process new information. In thinking back about the project our students did as a part of their study of the 1960s, I realized that just such an experience occurred. They formed teams to examine various aspects of the 1960s, such as the Vietnam War, the women's movement, and the changing attitudes of young people. They put notes in teachers' boxes asking them to share any memories they had of that era and found willing participants in the community who provided accounts more real and vivid than any in the textbook. Students watched old news clips, collected photographs, and read literature from that time period. One student found a woman who had been at Kent State the day of the fateful shootings, and the guest described in unforgettable detail a first-hand account of the events. We were all transported back in time as she spoke, visualizing the chaos and fear through her memories. The final reports, both written and oral, were the natural culmination of network learning; knowledge was transformed into a systemic event. At the time, I didn't consider the extenuating advantages, but in comparing the project to quality professional development, I am now able to recognize similar characteristics: relationships form, barriers of age disappear, attitudes and experiences converge, and an enriched environment supports independent and ongoing learning.

Leadership Teams and Study Groups

Leadership teams and study groups have replaced traditional professional development in many schools around the country. These collaborative groups reduce that familiar sense of isolationism and frustration teachers experience when they don't have the opportunity or time to discuss student needs and common challenges in the classroom. Study groups can become important support networks leading to an increased sense of community and professional friendships if they are valued and time is provided for them (as opposed to squeezing a study group into an already vacuum-packed schedule). Strong bonds help create a stimulating environment where thinking is challenged, confirmed, or expanded. Research shows that schools that engage in the practice of professional study groups experience long-term, specific benefits both for the staff and for the students, such as high levels of collegiality, innovation, and commitment (Murphy and Lick 2001, 45). The question, then, is why students are so often excluded from this powerful form of learning. The obsolete model of a knowledgeable one lecturing to less knowledgeable others no longer works, especially with a generation of students who can access the knowledge through a variety of engaging media any time they choose.

In your mind's eye, envision a school where student study groups meet simultaneously on a variety of topics. Consider student study group actions from the list below, or think about your own content area and list topics that you traditionally teach that would lend themselves to study group learning.

Content-Area Study Group Actions

◆ Read a contemporary novel that reflects Southern culture, such as *Fried Green Tomatoes, Cold Sassy Tree, The Secret Life of Bee,* or *The Color Purple.*

◆ Examine the changing use of grammar in the last fifty years, especially as it relates to popular culture, such as with advertising and instant messaging.

◆ Analyze the role of the Taliban in Middle Eastern affairs.

◆ Examine the long-term effects of the United States' unilateral intervention in the last decade.

◆ Study fault lines that could cause earthquakes.

◆ Evaluate alternative energy sources.

◆ Determine math and architectural skills necessary to design a new bridge (or other infrastructure) for the community.

◆ Read a biography of a record-setting sports figure.

◆ Examine modern tragic heroes in literature and/or film.

◆ Study the pine bark beetle and its widespread damage to U.S. forests

◆ Analyze different types of news media to determine bias.

◆ Predict how cars of the future will operate.

◆ Study depression and the debate over the use of antidepressants.

◆ Research the history of place value and numerations systems.

◆ Read books that span content areas, such as *Freakonomics: A Rogue Economist Explores the Hidden Side of Everything* (Levitt and Dubner).

Student study group topics should be publicized to the community in the local or school newspaper with times and dates for in-class study as well as any sessions that may be held outside of class. Community members, parents, and other teachers might be invited to attend as interest dictates, but students would form the core group. Core groups typically have 4-6 members; each student in the group should choose a role, which may be either set for the duration of the group or rotated based on the group's preference or needs. Students may also wish to share roles, such as having cofacilitators. Sample roles include:

◆ The facilitator keeps the meeting focused and makes sure each person's voice is heard by prompting discussion and dialogue. This person should be a good listener, well organized, and knowledgeable (or willing to become knowledgeable) about the topic of study. Facilitators should understand that they are not "in charge" in the traditional sense; they are, rather, the hub that keeps the wheel moving smoothly by ensuring that each person is a necessary and valuable part of the whole. Effective facilitators are team builders, not dictators.

◆ The recorder keeps accurate notes. A chart stand and chart for recording notes is a valuable tool that will allow each member to keep track of important points. The recorder will have the additional responsibility of making sure everyone has notes or summaries from the previous session and will keep a notebook of learning that will serve as a complete record of the group's study.

◆ The timekeeper keeps the group on task by reminding members of the agenda time frames, remaining time in the session, and upcoming deadlines. He or she will ensure that the meetings start and end on time.

◆ The researcher explores the answers to questions, brings new materials for the group to peruse, takes questions to the teacher, finds guests who may add to the study, and provides resources (such as websites, books, articles) as needed.

Other roles can be created based upon the makeup of the group. Students can become quite creative in finding tasks for everyone as members assume ownership of the group. Examples include a social chair (it'sespecially helpful if food is a part of the meeting), a logistics person if meetings take place after class, or a materials person in charge of handouts.

The group should form its own ground rules. Provide models such as the following:

◆ Everyone's voice will be heard and respected.

◆ No one will dominate the discussion. One person will talk at a time.

◆ The session will begin promptly and end at the arranged time.

◆ Everyone agrees to the assigned tasks (such as reading in-between meetings) so that the group time can be spent in discussion.

◆ Members will not engage in side conversations, but will direct comments to the entire group.

See Figure 10.1 for an example of a student study group meeting log.

Each member of the group should fill out an individual reflection log at the conclusion of the study group session (see Figure 10.2). These logs will be kept by participants in a notebook or portfolio and may be used by the teacher as the basis for participation grades or ongoing assessment, but, as always, intrinsic engagement in learning is the ultimate goal.

Student study groups, of course, can be as varied as the members of the group, but the following group categories may help a school or teacher get started with the process. As student study groups become an accepted and

Student Study Group Meeting Log

Topic: Date:

Text:

Facilitator:

Members Present:

Five-Minute Rewind: Facilitator and recorder review major points of discussion from last meeting.

Five-Minute Fast Forward: Facilitator reminds group of goals of study.

Group Action (to be completed by recorder with input from study group members):

1. What did members read or write to prepare for the meeting?

2. What major points did the group address in today's meeting? Summarize the content covered.

3. What new learning occurred today?

4. What questions emerged as a result of the dialogue?

5. Who will attempt to find answers to the questions?

6. What other resources (such as teachers, experts in field, books, websites) will be required to address questions for ongoing learning?

7. What will be the focus of the next meeting?

8. If additional materials or resources are needed, who will be responsible for bringing them to the next meeting?

9. What will members read or write in preparation for next meeting?

10. Best quotes from today's meeting: Write the quotes verbatim, giving credit to the author or speaker.

Additional Notes:

FIGURE 10.1

valued method of learning, students and teachers will begin to view topics and materials from the perspective of group learning. Once this type of schooling becomes ingrained, there will be no end to the variety and depth of learning.

Student Study Group
Individual Reflection Log

Name:

Topic of Study:

Date:

1. What did you learn from today's study?

2. Write one comment from a group member or from your reading that you want to remember.

3. Respond to the above. In what way did the quote teach you, inspire you, puzzle you, or affect you in any other way?

4. What more do you want to learn about today's topic?

5. How will you use what you learned or read?

Other comments or thoughts:

FIGURE 10.2

Sample Student Study Group Topics

Historical Events

Historical events instinctively appeal to students because of their background knowledge, which creates intrinsic interest. For example, when hundreds of thousands of adolescents saw the movie *Titanic*, they became interested in every aspect of the ship and the smallest detail surrounding its sinking. History, when *experienced*, can create almost obsessive engagement. Unfortunately, such events are often addressed superficially, distilled down to sterile dates and details, or eliminated due to time constraints, and students may never have an opportunity to kindle that initial interest. Other examples, such as the Lewis and Clark expedition, appeal to students who have visited the exhibition on display in museums around the country; the golden age of Harlem is riveting to those who have relatives living there. Other historical events of interest are the French Revolution; the death of the civil rights worker in Meridian, Mississippi, in 1964; the *Apollo* space mission; the Gulf War; the Salem witch trials; or the yellow fever epidemic. The trouble is that because students' background experiences are so varied and curriculum is so limited, teachers cannot address each student's interests in a one-curriculum-fits-all class.

Such a group is perfect for interdisciplinary study, as events can be tied to novels in English, historical eras in social studies, or topics in science. An added advantage of this type of group is that students learn how to study history in depth and find its relevance to their own lives instead of the traditional "unit" where they memorize facts but don't gain a true understanding of the human and societal factors that infuse historical events.

Primary Documents

Primary documents are inherently engaging to students because they make a connection that appeals to the senses. Glencoe, in collaboration with *Time* magazine, created a series of primary documents titled Moments in Time. The historical photographs, diary entries, song lyrics, artwork, political cartoons, and other relevant documents form a vivid and compelling mosaic of fifteen eras in U.S. history from George Washington to the war on terror. Students spend hours poring over the units. The power of the documents and the realization that they are staring history in the face elicits discussions and reflections from students that are spontaneous, genuine, and insightful.

Teachers and students can easily duplicate this idea by researching and studying primary documents for a variety of topics. Once students have acquired primary-based documents for a particular topic, they can put together their findings for other students to use in the future.

National Public Radio has a series titled Lost and Found Sound where they play sounds that correlate to events in the past, such as the recording of a man who recalled the day he heard Lincoln give the Gettysburg Address or the sounds of West Virginia steam trains (available on CD at www.lostand-foundsound.com). Such a program is a good starting place for students who want to study their world from a different perspective. *Poetry Speaks* (Paschen and Mosby 2001), a book that includes CDs of poetry recorded in the poet's own voice, from Walt Whitman to Billy Collins, is a mesmerizing resource for a poetry study group. Library archives, museums, websites, and bookstores contain all types of documents, such as videos, newspaper articles, photographs, journals, and recordings. Interviews and field trips are also valuable sources for collecting primary documents.

PBS is another rich storehouse for documentaries of events and figures who may not even be mentioned in textbooks. *Brother Outsider: The Life of*

Bayard Rustin, for example, is an award-winning documentary by film-makers Nancy Kates and Bennett Singer that tells the story of a civil rights activist who formulated many of the strategies that propelled the Civil Rights Movement. This documentary provides a fascinating look at a little-known piece of history. The film is available on the PBS website and schools can obtain it on VHS from California Newsreel (www.newsreel.org). This is only one of hundreds of PBS documentaries from music to history to current events that engage students in learning and deepen their knowledge at the same time.

Topics of Interest

Interdisciplinary study groups, like extracurricular clubs, are popular with all students, but especially with those who are not interested in joining the often cliquish social or service clubs. As with professional study groups, the administration should commit to the success of student study groups, making time and providing resources to support the meetings. An interdisciplinary study group often grows from a topic that is introduced in class, where the opportunity to fully plumb its depths is cut short because of a syllabus that demands a marching pace. Teenagers often meet peers in the cafés of their local bookstore, books and papers spread across coffee-stained tables, engaged in deep intellectual discussions. Such energetic gatherings can and should be a part of the school culture.

Topics should be submitted to a student leadership class, the student government association, or a teacher, perhaps the media specialist, willing to take on the job of organizing schoolwide study groups. Periodically, new groups should be announced with meeting times. Examples of topics that interest literally all students include string theory, civil rights, space, crimes, films, psychology topics, school/district-related issues (such as mandatory uniforms), or topics that include an activity, such as how to invest in the stock market or write a novel.

This type of study group needs access to supplemental texts, computers, and a well-stocked library, but that factor should not be a deterrent. Students or their parents will agree to purchase books to add to their own personal libraries, especially if given a choice about what they are studying, and community organizations or businesses will often donate funds for academic pursuits. Too often, knowledge is limited to a single textbook or books available in the school library, eliminating the latest, often most engaging, information related to content areas.

Book Clubs

Oprah's Book Club is the most famous, of course, but even Oprah couldn't have sold an idea that wasn't appealing to the masses. The concept of reading a book and sharing it with others is timeless, but somehow the English curriculum has turned the study of novels into a labyrinth of questions, one leading to another, as students negotiate answers to find their way out of a series of maddening assignments. Students need to learn to think, form their own opinions, make connections, and build background knowledge through interaction with others, not through study guides that reduce rich and thought-provoking literature to correct answers. In addition, we know that reading widely and often is an important factor in creating and engaging solid readers. Still, English classes across the nation are requiring that students read only books that are a part of an immovable canon. If teachers must insist on having students read their favorites, they at least should offer choices in the form of book clubs.

Schools or single classes can engage an entire community in the joy of reading by offering readers of all ages the opportunity to share the common experiences that resonate through good literature. In a high school English class where a group of students was reading *Fahrenheit 451*, a local attorney who loved the novel asked if he could join students as they were reading. Indeed, his insights and enthusiasm helped to create a memorable experience for these students. I have found that there are many members of the community who would be grateful for the chance to explore their favorite novels with a group of students, especially when students have chosen the book to study because they are interested in it, not because it is required reading.

Writing Groups

Writing is a process that requires practice and feedback. Unfortunately, too many teachers don't have the time, or in some cases the expertise, to help students as they struggle with composition. Other students have not experienced the fulfillment of writing because they see it only as a task that must be completed for a grade. Writing groups will meet the varying needs of students as well as adults, many of whom still feel less than confident in their writing abilities. Topics are endless: fiction, poetry, essay, research, technical writing, columns, narratives, science fiction, satire, even political cartoons. The newspaper or literary magazine staff could sponsor these study groups, or group members could meet without a sponsor for the sole purpose of reading each other's work and providing feedback for their writing. Editors from local newspapers are more than willing to become members of writing groups, adding valuable insights from their own careers in writing.

Science Research

Some schools provide a class in science research, often for the purpose of completing science projects for fairs. Increasingly, funding is not available for such classes or science teachers are asked to incorporate science fair projects into their standard curriculum. Schools that require students to complete a science project find that projects are duplicates of previous students' work or a brief exercise in science rather than a true learning experience. Study groups, then, either in class or after class, will provide a vehicle for those who want to delve into specific science topics such as astronomy, endangered species, water pollution, alternative fuel sources, erosion control, volcanic action, new diseases (such as West Nile virus), or biological pest control. Because learning in these groups is based on issues relevant to students' interests, the members become enthusiastic learners whose study may lead to science fair awards or influence their choice of schooling or careers. Once again, business or governmental agencies, such as local research labs or the Environmental Protection Agency, may have employees eager to join the group.

School Improvement Issues

Teachers who serve on school improvement and leadership teams meet regularly to address issues that significantly affect students. Sometimes the student government association or club presidents are invited to participate, but often decisions are made by the staff team and passed down to the students in the form of edicts. Such a lack of ownership in one of the most important parts of their lives creates the feeling in students that they are pawns in a game over which they have little control. Common challenges such as elective offerings, lunch schedules, parking problems, or disciplinary actions are ideal topics for a study group made up of staff members *and* students. In fact, the more complex the issue, the more students' perspectives are needed, as they are in a unique position to know the school in a way that adults may not have considered. Important decisions, such as whether or not to create a school-within-a school, adopt a new reading program, or spend funds on a new building, should include everyone's opinion, especially those for whom the benefit is intended. When schools include students in decision-making processes, students form a commitment to their school that results in long-term and tangible benefits.

College Credit

Although dual-enrolled classes are popular, consider a "class" of students and teachers enrolled in a college class offered at their school. If your local community college or university has a continuing education department, ask if they would be willing to offer courses at the school. Many students who are not ready (or don't have the necessary prerequisites) to take advantage of a dual-enrolled course are nevertheless eager to get a taste of college by participating in a course based on their interests. Topics such as art or music appreciation, psychology, or creative writing may interest faculty, parents, and community members as well. Bringing courses "home" to the school sends an important message that learning is accessible and ongoing, while providing a comfortable setting that invites students to discover the intrinsic rewards in extended learning.

Current Events

Students are interested in their world and the events that influence their daily and future lives. Once students actively and consistently begin reading, watching, or even paying attention to current events, they will become hooked as solidly as any adult news junkie. Much like nonfiction soap operas, news magazines provide the next episode in both human features and world events. A study group that meets weekly to explore current events will soon have more members than it can accommodate, breaking into current-event interest groups or groups inclined to a particular political leaning. Generic newsmagazines such as *Time, Newsweek,* or *U.S. News and World Report,* all available in online formats as well, are great places to begin, and student subscriptions are available at a reasonable cost. Online magazines such as *Salon* or *Wired News* are more avant-garde and appeal to those with a technology bent. Such a study group will also lead to activities that encourage interaction through blogs or bulletin boards. This type of study group, one that should be a part of every school, is vitally important if we believe that a comprehensive education includes allowing students the opportunity to practice civic responsibility by providing a glimpse into the world in which they will become keepers.

In what has become an information age, no one has exclusive rights to knowledge that is both ubiquitous and ever-changing. Knowledge is a commodity in a supply-and-demand society that is available to the masses, even those with little capital. The generations of students we are now teaching have become experts in the information market. Ironically, it is schools themselves, those age-old purveyors of knowledge, that are falling behind. If we are to engage these information-savvy students, we must embrace the concept that all learning, for teachers as well as students, is a socially constructed, ongoing, systemic process that requires the use and application of knowledge. To hold on to an obsolete method of learning can only spell the demise of our system of education; students *will* learn what they want and need to learn—with or without us.

11

Engagement Through Action Research

We have a hunger for the mind which asks for knowledge of
all around us, and the more we gain, the more is our desire;
the more we see, the more we are capable of seeing.

—MARIA MITCHELL

Writing as a way of knowing was my mantra as an English teacher,
and every student I ever taught had the opportunity to experience knowing in just that way. I provided ten minutes three
times a week for the practice of journal writing and found that most students came to treasure that time as one where they could hone their skills
as writers and discover something about themselves as intellectual beings
and thinkers. It was only when I was introduced to the concept of action
research that I began to have some persistent questions about this career-
long practice. The questions crept into my mind like those aggravating
microscopic insects, no-see-ums, that nibble on your skin on hot summer
evenings. How much did journal writing help students who needed specific
help with detail, conventions of writing, or mechanics? How much did journal writing help proficient writers who needed to spend time honing their
skill? Was thirty minutes a week too much time—or too little—for journaling? Did the practice of journal writing transfer to other writing, such
as creative or expository writing? Did having my students write for only
ten minutes per session encourage superficiality? Action research would
have helped me find the answers to such questions and provide my students the best type of help with their writing.

My research might have looked something like this:

Focus Question (often called the more formal "research question")

◆ Does journal writing thirty minutes a week improve students' skills as writers?

Data Related to the Question

◆ surveys and interviews with students asking them how writing in journals affects their overall writing ability

◆ comparison of writing from "case study" students at the beginning of the year and after writing in journals for several months

◆ comparison of the writing from two sets of students: those who have journaled in class and those who have not

◆ comparison of writing from three sets of students: those who write thirty minutes a week, those who write fifty minutes a week, and those who write ten minutes a week in journals

◆ standardized test scores of students who have written in journals and students who have not

◆ survey of students' teachers asking them if they see a difference in the writing skills of students who have spent time journaling compared to those who have not

◆ Articles, books, and research related to journal writing

Analyzing the Data

◆ What does the data tell me about my focus question?

◆ Can I draw a conclusion about the benefit of having students write in journals based on the data I collected, or do I need more data to make a decision?

◆ If there is no definite answer, what have I learned that will improve my practice regarding journal writing?

Action Based on Findings

◆ Will I increase or decrease the time students will write in journals, or have students continue to write thirty minutes per week?

◆ How will I continue to monitor the benefits of student journal writing?

◆ Are there other areas that I might alter, such as the prompts?

◆ Will I decide to engage my peers and/or students in a study group that examines journaling in more depth, perhaps using *The Journal Book* (Fulwiler 1987) as a source?

Action research doesn't have to be a formalized procedure; it can start with asking a question—or, as in my case, many questions—about an instructional practice or a pedagogical problem, and end with an informed decision about how to best help students learn. Many current action research projects involve literacy concerns, such as why students often read well orally but can't comprehend what they are reading. Such challenges are complex and varied, so a systematic way of addressing the problem based on individual student data is the best way to arrive at an accurate answer. Using only standardized test scores to make decisions about instruction inevitably does more harm than good.

Action research is also an effective method to solve problems facing entire schools. A high school in northern Florida, for example, lost many of its faculty members and almost half of its student body to a new high school built in a nearby community. It was becoming clear that the old school would struggle to survive, with few resources and little funding to keep it running. The faculty, student body, and administration faced the literal demise of their school. After brainstorming possible solutions to save the school, the faculty decided that a viable solution was to create magnet programs within the school that would attract students from around the district, increasing the student population and thus bringing in additional revenue. The faculty wisely began collecting data before taking action. They surveyed their student body to find out what type of magnet programs would be appealing to them and discovered that their students were interested in programs that already existed in the school, such as drama, law, art, and music. They then contacted schools around the nation with similar populations of students that had developed magnet programs. The staff determined that they needed more information to make the best decision and appealed to the school board for funds to investigate further. They were granted enough money for groups of staff members to observe schools with programs similar to the ones their students had expressed an interest in attending.

They found a school with a state-of-the-art dance studio, a school whose music program included guitar and keyboarding, and a law academy that attracted students interested in prelaw as well as criminal justice and law enforcement. The teachers now had a vision of what their school could become and how much it would cost to turn their vision into reality. They took the plan back to the student body and faculty, tweaked some details, and began the process of generating funding for their dream.

Today the school is a firmly established magnet center that draws students from all over the city as well as from surrounding counties. The drama department boasts a costume and makeup class, the law program recently built a law library with donations from local attorneys, and the dance studio is beautiful—its mirror-lined walls and shiny practice bars reflecting dancers whirling to ballet, jazz, and modern dance music.

This cycle is an action research classic: A focus question emerged based on need, data was collected and analyzed, and a solution was proffered. Now hundreds of students' lives have been changed by a process of learning that rarely fails.

Student-Centered Action Research

If such a dynamic and effective process can generate these amazing results, why isn't this tool offered to students in every class? For several years, study skills classes were requirements for many secondary students throughout the country. While some of the classes were undoubtedly beneficial, others were merely holding tanks where students were given a series of worksheets on how to study, how to take notes, and how to use a dictionary. The course had a misplaced focus; students should have been given opportunities to inquire, discover, hypothesize, and revise their thinking, both about content-area topics and about their own learning through action research.

The purpose of student-driven action research is for students to develop a sense of inquiry that will remain with them throughout their lives. Action research may take an entire semester to complete, may be ongoing into the next course, or may conclude within a few days, depending upon the complexity of the topic and the time it takes to collect and analyze data. It is a *method* of thinking that creates an interactive relationship between the learner and the content, one that becomes an inherent part of every type of learning.

The best action research topics arise as a part of in-class study. Teachers should create an action research board where students post topics they would like to investigate. Then, students explore the topics in "action research" terms—seeing a question mark behind each thought. They should also learn to question assertions presented by textbooks and teachers. Students should come to understand that there may not be a single answer;

it is the process of asking the question, not the definitive answer, where the greatest learning lies.

Spending time on constructing the focus question is time well spent. Good research questions:

◆ should be meaningful to students, something they want to investigate;

◆ should be neither so broad that the research will be frustrating nor so narrow that there are few options for researching;

◆ should reflect everyday challenges, such as how to find the least expensive automobile insurance or discovering careers that will best suit students' interests and talents; and

◆ should focus on ways that students find out about themselves as learners. Students often say, "I'm no good at . . . " when they should be asking, "Why am I not good at . . . ?" or "How can I become better at . . . ?" Students can learn the content better by finding out *how* they learn math or science or English.

Focus questions, then, should be reflective as well as content-specific. A reflective question has a metacognitive component, addressing how the student learns the subject. A content-specific question focuses on discovering more about the topic itself. Reflective action research questions:

◆ address individual learning;

◆ consider methods students can use to enhance content area learning; and

◆ probe how the content-area knowledge will affect students in their roles as future citizens.

In contrast, content-specific research questions:

◆ address specific topics of study;

◆ consider questions within that topic; and

◆ probe the topic for use and application.

Have students brainstorm topics for study individually and in small groups, considering the depth and type of research they need to conduct to find answers to their questions. Encourage them to take their time and talk with you, other students, or their parents about their questions. Once they have decided upon a topic, have them write the question as clearly and simply as possible. Sample action research questions, listed by subject area, follow.

English

Reflective Questions

◆ How can I increase my vocabulary?

◆ Is rhyming poetry easier for me to understand and/or appreciate than non-rhyming poetry?

Content-Area Questions

◆ In what way is the tragic hero of Greek drama replicated in current U.S. literature or films?

◆ What common characteristics do award-winning novels possess?

Reading

Reflective Questions

◆ How does fluency affect my comprehension?

◆ How did my early experiences with reading contribute to the type of reader I have become?

Content-Area Questions

◆ How can young adult novels be categorized to meet the interests and/or needs of various readers?

◆ How does informational text differ from fiction?

Science

Reflective Questions

◆ If the population continues to grow at its present rate, how will such growth affect the quality of my life as an adult?

◆ How might (a certain disease) affect my life or the lives of those I care about in the future?

Content-Area Questions

◆ What would be the effect of a meltdown at a nuclear power plant?

◆ How does ozone depletion affect the frequency and types of skin cancer?

Math

Reflective Questions

◆ Why are word problems (or equations) more difficult for me than other types of math?

◆ What type of instruction (practice, examples) best helps me understand math?

Content-Area Questions

◆ How do the sizes and shapes of modern structures compare to earlier "buildings" such as the pyramids?

◆ How does the use of statistical analysis improve modern daily life?

Social Studies

Reflective Questions

◆ Are my political leanings are toward conservatism or liberalism?

◆ How might outsourcing affect my future career opportunities?

Content-Area Questions

◆ What effect will the elimination of social security have on the national economy?

◆ What could the government do to assist native populations in maintaining their cultural traditions?

PE

Reflective Questions

◆ Historically, what practices contribute to a football (soccer, basketball) team's success?

◆ What variables contribute to my increased (or decreased) performance in sports?

Content-Area Questions

◆ How does mental imaging improve the performance of athletes?

◆ How widespread is the use of steroids in major league athletes?

Once students have formulated a question, they should post the question for everyone to see to encourage collaborative learning. Since the question is authentic and students have choice and ownership over the topic, they will become engaged in finding an answer—the action research process—and will naturally include others who might have something to offer. I have seen such collaboration form authentic learning partnerships and communities that sustain in-depth learning. Discuss the action research process, detailed below, including the process versus product nature of action research.

The Action Research Process

1. Generate a focus question that you are genuinely interested in exploring, one that will require "digging" to find an answer.

2. Collect data to be analyzed. Attorneys, researchers, and nonfiction writers use the concept of triangulation to arrive at a conclusion. That means they examine several pieces of data, often three, although that is not a magic number. Each piece of data tells a story, adds a piece that fills in the puzzle, and provides a clue to answer the focus question. Anything that provides accurate information can be a data source, including:

    ◆ interviews with those knowledgeable about the topic

    ◆ surveys, questionnaires

    ◆ reputable articles, books, or websites

    ◆ the textbook used by your class and others by different companies

    ◆ case studies

    ◆ portfolios of past work

    ◆ videos or recordings

    ◆ writing samples, math problems, journal entries, narratives

    ◆ records, research, or statistics

    ◆ physical artifacts

3. Organize the data by creating a system that works for you, according to date, similarities, differences, type, or chronology. Use folders, baskets, notebooks, or tape data to a wall in a continuum or chart form.

4. Analyze data by examining each piece and deciding how it provides a clue to your focus question. Jot down notes and look for the unexpected. Ask others to help you see the data with objective eyes:

- What does each piece of data reveal?

- In what way does it provide insight or information related to the focus question?

- What unexpected information did I uncover? What does it tell me?

- Do I see a pattern from which I can create a hypothesis?

5. Form an answer to your question. Don't be afraid to create a hypothesis that may not be definitive. The goal isn't necessarily to find the right answer; it is, rather, to test the answer you have come up with based on reliable data. Discovering what does not support your hypothesis is as important as finding out what does.

6. Decide what, if any, action needs to be taken to address the focus question. You may need to collect more data or your research may simply lead you to an increased understanding of your question.

Action research projects should be a significant part of the school, district, and community's archives. When students find satisfactory answers to focus questions, the results should be published in the local newspaper or on the internet, shared at school board meetings, and placed in libraries so that the knowledge is available for others who are seeking similar answers.

Action research is a close friend to study groups. When schools and individual classes use these two powerful tools, learning will shift from what is often a passive endeavor to an engaging, collaborative process. More importantly, such a process will become an intrinsic part of how students and teachers come to view learning—as an act embedded in inquiry, discovery, reflection, and action. The deep satisfaction inherent in such accomplishment will meet the needs of brains searching for meaning and learners searching for validation.

12

Learning Through Coaching

Our tendency to reduce teaching to questions of technique is one
reason we lack a collegial conversation of much duration or depth.

—PARKER PALMER, *THE COURAGE TO TEACH*

For ten years I cotaught with a social studies teacher, and it was one
of the best experiences of my career. We learned with and from our
students and came to rely on each other as sounding boards for
ideas, collaborators for new curriculum, and counselors at the end of a bad
day. We were both in the room for a two-hour block every day with the same
students and the class flowed seamlessly. It wasn't a "his turn/my turn"
type of thing. My team teacher, Ben Dykema, taught social studies, and I
wove English into the class. When our students read *Animal Farm*, Ben
taught them about the Russian Revolution; when he taught a unit on the
Depression, I introduced Steinbeck.

Each week *Time* magazine became the deep well of our curriculum as we
tapped from it authentic, relevant, and purposeful vocabulary, writing
prompts, and topics for critical thinking. Its wide variety of photographs,
articles, essays, charts, and short takes made it the perfect medium for
meeting students' individual interests and expanding everyone's background knowledge. As savvy critics of current events, students also began
engaging their parents and other teachers, as well as their peers, in provocative discussions of world events. We supplemented their reading with real-
world experiences and field trips related to our study. Each year we took
students to Montgomery, Alabama, and toured the downtown church where
Martin Luther King, Jr. had first pastored, and students stood in awe behind

the podium where he began living his dream. Experiencing those tumul-tuous days in the birthplace of the Civil Rights Movement created an indeli-bility that is difficult to duplicate in a classroom. On the five-hour ride home, the study continued as groups of students took turns moving to the front of the bus where Ben and I sat. We engaged in long discussions about a Civil Rights Movement that was now as real as the seat beneath them. We helped them see with new eyes.

Our class resembled a yearlong study group, and the relationships that were forged among the students and with us were one of the most impor-tant aspects of the study. It wasn't until years later that I discovered that our coteaching was something that is now the latest trend in education. The word *coaching* is on the lips of administrators, reading teachers, and many students. Many schools, both elementary and secondary, now have in-house coaches—peers, as opposed to administrators, who work *with* teachers to help them improve their knowledge and their craft. Laura Robb describes a coach as one who "supports the teachers' explorations of a sub-ject by listening, observing, posing questions, conversing, and suggesting books and journal articles that can enlarge and extend the teacher's knowl-edge. The primary goal is to build on what a teacher knows and does well" (2000, 60). Robb lists guidelines for coaches that include:

- Listens well.
- Offers choices.
- Asks thought-provoking questions.
- Accepts the teacher where she or he is and gently moves her or him forward.
- Builds on what a teacher does well. Stresses the positive, yet offers suggestions for growth.
- Maintains confidentiality. Builds trust through negotiation, choices, shared study, and conversation.
- Helps teachers become reflective and self-evaluative.

Ben and I practiced those guidelines with each other without once knowing they were a formula for coaching. Our relationship of trust and unwavering respect for students led to what I remember as a near-perfect teaching and learning experience, and students have contacted us throughout the years to tell us that they thought so, too.

While the educational world is abuzz with coaching strategies, I sug-gest that coaching, as the word implies, is as natural as forming a friend-ship with someone you trust for advice and support. Teachers coach each other by talking, listening, observing, making suggestions, encouraging, and building an honest relationship. How are those interactions different from the relationship that a teacher hopes to engender with a student—or a student hopes to form with another student? When I sponsored the school newspaper, editors from one year coached the upcoming editors, working closely beside them as they brainstormed article ideas, edited articles, laid out pages, and offered tips and advice, both verbally and through a notebook that was passed from one editor to the next. Although I was there to facilitate the learning, it was the transmission of knowledge from one student to another that created real learning.

Coaching, in its purest form, is perfected from the human touch, something that computers can't duplicate and rubrics can't assess. It is an intuitive interaction among humans that leads to a deep synergy and satisfying connectedness, characteristics that beat within the heart of all good relationships.

Since that time, I have had other coaching relationships that I didn't identify as such. My close friend and editor, Gloria Pipkin, provides bull's eye suggestions for my writing, helping me find ways to improve and strengthen my skills; my colleague Susan Kelly spends hours talking with me about literacy and engagement, forcing my thinking deeper, leading me to possibilities I hadn't considered; my father, with his engineering mind, prods me by asking pointed questions that force me to think outside my teacher box; and my husband-coach, Bert, listens patiently as I read chapters aloud—often more than once—and lovingly encourages me. Their comments support, expand, and deepen my learning. A major component of my coaching is that I trust all of these people and value their input. They may not always be right, but they always cause me to reflect, to question, to grow as a writer and thinker. I often feel like a trapeze artist trying new moves high above the ground with my coaches far below calling out what they see from different perspectives—but stretching out that safety net just in case.

If, as a learner, such support is so important to my own development, I wince to think that education often doesn't provide that same sense of safety and encouragement for students. Although the best teachers have always acted as coaches to students, prodding, encouraging, challenging them to learn more, students also need peers as a part of their trusted community to help them with this messy business of learning.

One semester when I was in high school, I was assigned to a study hall. In this very large class, some students studied, some slept, but no one talked. Back then, study required silence and the teacher either didn't believe Vygotsky when he said that learning is socially constructed (1996) or she had never heard of him and his theories. Now, thirty years later, many schools act as if they, too, have not heard about research that confirms how important dialogue and social interaction are for conceptual understanding.

A Culture of Coaching

While study halls may not exist in many schools anymore, why not coaching halls? Schools have found innovative ways to create classes that meet their needs: test prep centers (in one school called a "success center"), computer labs, and a variety of special classes, such as leadership, academic literacy, research, study skills, senior projects, and tutoring. I propose that schools embrace the concept of full-scale coaching as a primary method of learning and find ways to provide time for teachers and students to practice coaching. Whether schools create informal coaching areas during lunch or before and after school, or more formal coaching classes in which students can enroll, the message will be clear: This is a school where learning communities are valued.

The study group format is one option available to students and teachers wishing to explore this method of learning, while others may need or prefer one-on-one coaching. In a school that adopts a culture of coaching, students and teachers become immersed in coaching as a natural way of learning with and from each other. Of course, in lieu of whole school coaching, teachers in individual classrooms or in conjunction with other teachers could easily institute the practice with their own students.

Just as sports coaches must *know* the sport, as well as the team members, to become winning coaches, academic coaches must first understand the process of learning before attempting to coach another about how to learn. They must believe that each learner has inherent strengths, as evidenced by Howard Gardner's work on multiple intelligences (1993). A school that adopts the coaching model should incorporate Brian Cambourne's conditions for learning as its mission statement, as ingrained as the alma mater or the best pep rally cheer.

During the first week of the coaching class all students should spend time examining theories regarding how they learn. It is also important for students to understand that intelligence is not fixed. The following provides an outline for such a class.

Learning About Learning

Cambourne's Conditions for Learning

◆ Students will describe their best learning experiences, inside or outside of school, and discuss how their experiences follow Cambourne's model.

◆ In groups, students will create a graphic illustration of Cambourne's conditions that shows how each condition interacts with the other. Students may utilize a variety of graphic organizers, employ symbolic representations, or create a collage using magazine pictures or their own drawings. Encourage students to include examples of their learning in their representations and put the final product on chart paper or poster board. Post all charts and have each group explain their ideas to the entire class.

Multiple Intelligences

◆ Ask students to respond to the following statement from Howard Gardner: "It is fundamentally misleading to think about a single mind, a single intelligence, a single problem-solving capacity" (2003, 13). Brainstorm different types of intelligences and ask which ones have traditionally been valued in school. Depending upon their answers, ask students if they think individuals can have a digital, compassionate, spiritual, or attention intelligence.

◆ Present to students each of Howard Gardner's eight intelligences: linguistic, logical-mathematical, musical, bodily-kinesthetic, spatial, interpersonal, intrapersonal, and naturalist. (See www.infed.org /thinkers/gardner.htm for a detailed explanation of each of the intelligences.) Have students list what they believe to be their top three strongest intelligences, pointing out that everyone, to some degree, possesses each of the intelligences.

◆ Have students examine the work of Howard Gardner. Middle school students will find the website "Concept to the Classroom" helpful, specifically the workshop that taps into multiple intelligences: www .thirteen.org/edonline/concept2class/mi/index.html. High schools students can download Gardner's answers to commonly asked questions as well as his section titled "Students Conducting Research" from www .howardgardner.com. Teachers will find other links at the same website that address classroom application of multiple intelligences and may wish to read his paper "Multiple Intelligences After Twenty Years," presented at the American Educational Research Association in 2003, also accessible through the website. Gardner recommends the book *Multiple Intelligences* (Kornhaber, Fierros, and Veenema 2004) for educators.

◆ Designate areas of the room labeled with each of the "intelligences." Ask students to go to the area that they believe names their strongest intelligence. Together, have them brainstorm on chart paper their favorite activities and least favorite activities as a springboard for discussion. They may wish to include other favorites as a comparison, such as favorite foods, favorite books or movies, favorite subjects in school. Then, ask them to move to their second and then third strongest intelligence, again discussing similarities and differences with their peers.

Creating a Learning Profile

◆ Point out that everyone learns in different ways based on the purpose and topic, as well as the learner's interests and background knowledge. Ask students how preference of learning—commonly designated as auditory, visual, and kinesthetic—fit into their overall learning profile. Brainstorm all the factors that might contribute to learning, such as experience, a supportive environment, or specific organizational techniques.

◆ Have students think about a learning experience they have had in the past that was difficult for them. Ask them to write about how they learned or, if they feel the learning was not successful, why not. Allow them to form groups and discuss their experiences.

◆ Using the factors for learning that students brainstormed earlier, have them create their own learning continuum where they place learning factors on a line, zero to ten. Zero indicates the factor does not have to be present in order for the student to learn effectively, ten indicates that it must be present. Factors may include noise, structure, authority figure present, motivation, or working in groups, to name a few. The purpose of this activity is for students to reflect on their own learning—often referred to as *metacognition*. Post the continuums as a reminder that everyone learns differently.

Once students have considered their own learning profile, they can plan for coaching. Coaching, scaffolded by conditions for learning, is the process of supporting others in their learning by providing the most basic of human interactions. Tell students that there is no magic formula for coaching; it is simply the application of good "people skills," or what is referred to as emotional quotient (EQ). Effective coaches listen attentively and carefully, ask questions both for clarification and for increased understanding, demonstrate or model when necessary, and provide authentic feedback. Students and teachers may be interested in reading "The EQ Factor" in *Time* magazine for a detailed look at how an individual's emotions, not his or her IQ, is a significant factor for success.

Coaching Classes

Teachers who facilitate coaching classes should first engage in studying professional materials related to coaching, such as Irene Fountas and Gay Pinnell's chapters in *Systems for Change* (Lyons and Pinell 2001) or Laura Robb's book *Redefining Staff Development: A Collaborative Model for Teachers and Administrators* (2000). The National Council of Teachers of English has also published a comprehensive resource on study groups and coaching (see www.ncte.org).

Coaching classes will allow students to have the experience both of being coached and of coaching, depending upon their strengths and needs. The bottom line is that students and teachers learn to become good coaches by coaching. Following are some practice exercises that hone coaching skills.

Practice Listening

Have the coach listen to the peer coach (at least 3-5 minutes) without saying a word. Provide talking and listening prompts for practice, such as the following:

◆ Describe a class in which you have learned a great deal. What made this class better than others?

◆ How would you describe yourself as a learner in first grade? Sixth? Ninth?

◆ What subject in school is most difficult for you?

Practice Objectivity

Good coaches don't judge or criticize. Give students magazine pictures or advertisements and have them tell their peer coach everything they see in the picture. Ask the coach to let his partner know if he begins to interpret rather than objectively state what is in the picture. Have students watch a television show or observe a teacher in a class and write down only what they see and hear without making any value judgements.

Practice Encouragement

Choose one student each day to be the recipient of encouragement. Everyone in the class will write a brief note to the designated student telling her something they admire about her academically. It may be how she answers questions thoughtfully, how smart she is in math, or that she is a good writer. All the notes go into a large brown envelope and are given to the student at the end of class.

Practice Coaching

Have each student bring one coaching issue to the class. For example, if a student's question is "How can I become better at organizing my essays?" or "Why can't I seem to understand word problems in math?" a student coach will practice coaching in front of the class. Other members of the class will take objective notes and discuss the interaction together.

Practice Using Prompts

The purpose of coaching is to prompt reflection, not to do the work for the learner. Since questioning and reflection are hallmarks of coaching, practice using these prompts until you become adept at the coaching process.

- What about this (problem, topic, assignment) is difficult for you?
- What about this (problem, topic, assignment) makes sense to you?
- How can I help you with this (problem, topic, assignment)?
- What do you want to accomplish?
- How can I help you practice _____?
- What do you want to try first?
- Let's just talk this through . . . .
- Can you summarize what you understand about the topic?
- When does the (confusion, difficulty, challenge) begin to appear?
- Would it help for me to do an example first?
- I have trouble (learning, doing, trying) _____, and this helps me when I get stuck . . . .

◆ How can you apply your strengths to this (problem, topic, assignment)?

◆ Would it help if we read the text together?

◆ Knowing your own learning style, how could you look at this (problem, topic, assignment) from another perspective?

◆ Look at this method of organization and see if it makes sense to you.

◆ I know that you can do this. We just have to find what works for you.

◆ Do you need me to help you find other (texts, resources) that might explain the content in another way?

◆ Would you like help in coming up with a list of questions to take to the teacher?

◆ I'll listen while you explain in your own words . . . .

Practice Using Data

Encourage students to bring samples of work to the practice coaching sessions. Students who want help organizing essays could bring an essay they are writing; students who want help with math problems could bring sample math problems.

Practice Analyzing Coaching Sessions

Videotape coaching sessions so students in the class can deconstruct the interaction and learn from it. Remind them that there is no right way and that different coaches may approach the issue differently. The point is to prompt self-reflection and move the student being coached to a better understanding of his own learning.

> STUDENT: My teacher always says that my essays are disorganized, but I don't know *how* to make them more organized.

> COACH: Let's look at one of your essays and list the order in which you presented your ideas.

> STUDENT: Well, first I said . . . .

> COACH: Why did you decide to put that point first?

> STUDENT: It seemed to be the most important point.

> COACH: What came after that?

> STUDENT: I explained that . . . .

> COACH: And then what?

STUDENT: Well, I next said . . . .

COACH: Does this point seem to logically follow the last point? What if you added this here . . . .

STUDENT: Yes, I could do it that way, but how will I know on my own the best way to organize my ideas? I can't seem to tell what should come first and then next. I just write as it comes to me.

COACH: Maybe if you talked through your points first that would help you see how they relate to each other.

A coaching class should be a safe environment to practice coaching and to internalize the concept that helping each other through dialogue and feedback is invaluable in the learning process.

Not all students will have the academic background or knowledge to help peers with their learning. I would have a difficult time coaching someone with a calculus problem, but I may be able to help him unravel the problem for himself by asking the right questions, or help him identify what he doesn't understand so he can confidently approach the teacher for help. Ask students to consider their strengths in one of three coaching areas, described below, which, of course, will vary according to the coaching situation. (See also Figure 12.1 for examples of coach behaviors.)

Content Coach

This coach focuses on helping another student gain knowledge, increase understanding, or improve skills. Such a coach has an affinity for a certain subject area, such as equations or writing, and helps another student or group of students with specific content-area topics. For example, considering the current trend toward literacy coaches, students could easily assist in this role by listening to their peers read and coaching them in activating background knowledge, visualizing, or paying attention to text features. In addition, they could partner-read, discuss shared books, or show reluctant readers their own metacognitive processes for approaching difficult text. I am convinced that such an individual coaching relationship would do more toward helping reluctant readers than all the commercial reading programs rolled into one.

The beauty of this type of coaching is that everyone has an area of expertise—sports, music, art, academic subjects—and, thus, at some point will have the credentials for becoming a coach. In addition, the one who is the coach one day becomes the one being coached the next day, depending upon individual learning needs. This type of coach, following Cambourne's

Behaviors of Student Coaches

Student coaches:	Student coaches *do not:*
Prompt for reflection	Have all the answers
Probe for depth	Lecture
Encourage success	Act insincere or dishonest
Listen actively	Dominate the conversation
Allow for autonomy	Take over
Act as a trusted friend	Criticize
Remain objective	Become judgmental
Learn with their coaching peer	Act as a teacher
Ask questions	Demand answers
Seek to understand	Expect compliance

FIGURE 12.1

conditions, *demonstrates* new learning and provides "relevant, appropriate, timely, readily available, and nonthreatening, with no strings attached" (1995, 187) responses. The coach understands the importance of an environment where the learner must feel safe to take risks and make mistakes, so one of his most important roles is to be standing by as the learner practices and develops control over his learning task.

Process Coach

This coach is a logistical dream, helping students who feel comfortable with the content area but have difficulty applying new knowledge or getting what they know into the required format. Students who have a knack for organization coach those who need help with such things as the mechanics of polishing a paper, including help with grammar and spelling, effective notetaking procedures, organizing notebooks, portfolios, or lab notes. Such coaches understand *how* to get things done efficiently and aid those who understand the content but are a bit scattered. Many students want to take responsibility for their learning, an essential condition, but they have difficulty deciding what, how, and when to learn. Often, very bright students who have a firm grip on the subject can't arrange, categorize, or systematize the information—and others are naturals at these skills. By helping such learners acquire and maintain responsibility over what they know, these coaches play a vital role in the learning process.

Encouragement Coach

This "cheerleader" coach is best at encouragement, helping others understand and appreciate their strengths. The coach assists the learner in forming "high, realistic expectations that he can and will succeed." These coaches may not need to have a firm grasp on the content, but they have such strong interpersonal intelligence that they are able to help learners gain confidence as they attempt new learning. They generally have an optimistic nature and are good at listening, asking questions, and offering positive feedback. This type of coach would be perfect for performance classes, such as drama, debate, or courses requiring presentations, such as a senior project class.

All coaches, students and teachers, should take into consideration the following tips:

◆ Ask how you can help before offering suggestions.

◆ Allow enough time and space for coaching peers to think.

◆ Seek the teacher's help or outside resources if you need help.

◆ See yourself as a colearner, not as one who will "teach" the other.

◆ Practice patience. Everyone has strengths and challenges.

◆ Avoid asking yes or no questions.

◆ Ask questions you may not be able to answer.

◆ Suggest articles, websites, or books related to the topic.

◆ Stay on task and try to be aware when you are distracting rather than facilitating.

◆ Make a pledge of confidentiality and trust.

◆ Don't judge or criticize your coaching peer under any circumstance.

◆ If the match doesn't work, back out of the partnership.

◆ Celebrate successes, no matter how small.

Many secondary schools note that their students and faculty lack a sense of community, resulting in a loss of cohesiveness and empathy. Classes are too large, students form cliques, and disinterest is widespread.

Coaching will serve to diminish many of these systemic problems as students come to know and rely on each other by forming a culture of trust. The research on schools within schools has demonstrated that students benefit academically and socially in an environment that is structured to meet their individual needs and foster relationships. As students learn to cope in an increasingly complex society, they will need the skills that coaching develops—perhaps more than the knowledge that schools are so desperately hoping to instill.

Coda

It is the supreme art of the teacher to awaken
joy in creative expression and knowledge.

—ALBERT EINSTEIN

The concept of engaging adolescents in learning is not
new. Educators have been struggling with the idea,
along with its companion, motivation, since the turn
of the twentieth century. John Dewey wrote in 1933,

> Mere facts or data are dead, as far as mind is con-
> cerned, unless they are used to suggest and test some
> idea, some way out of difficulty. Ideas, on the other
> hand, are *mere* ideas, ideal speculations, fantasies,
> dreams, unless they are used to guide new observa-
> tions of, and reflections upon, actual situations, past,
> present, or future.

Dewey could be describing a classroom where facts and
ideas are the window dressings and students are manne-
quins. Engagement requires a transformation of the facts
and ideas into action. Classrooms themselves have morphed
throughout the years with the addition of what appears to
be increasing engagement (videos, charts, brightly colored
texts, computer programs) but the vital component of engagement—the action, not the accoutrements of engagement—
is missing. If students don't apply facts and ideas to reflect,
consider, speculate, imagine, probe, test, and reinvent in a

151

safe environment that encourages such cognitive activities, they are not learners, they are voyeurs.

It was the last day of school for high school English teacher Nancy Goodwin. Before she left for the year, she took the time to email me her reflections:

> Well, I made it again. The way I teach is always a risk that I wrestle with, knowing there's a gamble in trusting that students, given the opportunity, will really use the time offered for reading, reflection, and connected writing. Some of the kids used it well and had worthwhile dialogues with themselves, yet others never or rarely seemed to become engaged in a very meaningful way. Some can't seem to even figure out what that means. Tragically, many students don't see themselves as intellectual beings, don't know how to initiate critical thinking or internal dialogue beyond the surface of everyday stuff; they don't seem to live the "examined life" in which writing comes naturally or where reading has much of a place. Perhaps part of the problem is that traditionally we've done so much of their thinking for them. We ask the questions; we tell them what to read; we suggest or require certain topics; we give the vocabulary lists. They are always processing what is already provided for them. THEY need to learn to ask the questions, choose the reading, initiate the topics; discover their own vocabulary, develop an intellectual momentum of their own that feeds itself and grows thereby. I know that is the magic that needs to happen. I DON'T always know how to make it happen when students' intellectual curiosity has been dulled and stunted by years of worksheets and multiple-choice tests. I realize the solution to issues of nonengagment isn't one-dimensional, for the causes are societal and numerous and not just the result of unsound educational practices, but I do know that figuring out the answers to this essential question is at the heart of success for my students and for me. (personal communication, May 2005)

Brian Cambourne has provided a model for engagement that involves action, and I have provided activities that build upon the actions he suggests, but it is really the underlying belief that students *must* have the freedom to learn in ways that make sense to them that will lead to engagement. There is no scientific formula, no silver bullet, no beautifully packaged programs that will guarantee engagement. Engagement, the factor that is at the center of all learning, resides within each of us. Together, as we continue to ask the questions and form synergistic relationships in pursuit of the answers, engagement will emerge to support us as we discover and transform knowledge.

References

AMEN, DANIEL. 2003. *Healing ADD.* New York: G. P. Putnam's Sons.

BODROVA, ELENA, and DEBORAH LEONG. 1996. *Tools of the Mind: The Vygotskian Approach to Early Childhood Education.* Upper Saddle River, NJ: Prentice-Hall.

BROOKS, JACQUELINE, and MARTIN BROOKS. 1999. *In Search of Understanding: The Case for Constructivist Classrooms.* Alexandria, VA: Association for Supervision and Curriculum Development.

CAMBOURNE, BRIAN. 1988. *The Whole Story: Natural Learning and the Acquisition of Literacy in the Classroom.* New York: Scholastic.

———. 1995. "Toward an Educationally Relevant Theory of Literacy Learning: Twenty Years of Inquiry." *The Reading Teacher* 49 (November): 182-190.

COLES, GERALD. 2004. "Danger in the Classroom: 'Brain Glitch' Research and Learning To Read." *Phi Delta Kappan* 85 (January): 344-351.

DEWEY, JOHN. 1986. "How We Think: A Restatement of the Relation of Reflective Thinking to the Educative Process." In J. A. Boydston (ed.), *John Dewey: The Later Works, 1925-1953* (Vol. 8, pp. 105-352). Carbondale, IL: Southern Illinois University Press (Original work published 1933).

DONSKY, PAUL. "Desperate Schoolteachers: Under Pressure for Their Students to Perform Well on National Tests, Some Georgia Teachers Break the Rules." *Atlanta Journal Constitution* 15 May 2005: A1+.

FULWILER, TOBY, ed. 1987. *The Journal Book.* Portsmouth, NH: Boynton Cook.

GARDNER, HOWARD. 1983, 1993. *Frames of Mind: The Theory of Multiple Intelligences.* New York: Basic Books.

———. "Multiple Intelligences After Twenty Years." American Educational Research Association. Chicago, Illinois. 21 April 2003.

GIBBS, NANCY. "The EQ Factor." *Time* 2 October 1995. http://www.time.com/time/classroom/psych/unit5_article1.html.

GUSKEY, THOMAS. 2000. *Evaluating Professional Development.* Thousand Oaks, CA: Corwin.

GUTHRIE, JOHN, and DONNA ALVERMANN, eds. 1999. *Engaged Reading: Processes, Practices, and Policy Implications.* New York: Teachers College Press.

HAMMOND, LINDA DARLING, and GARY SYKES, eds. 1999. *Teaching as the Learning Profession: Handbook of Policy and Practice.* San Francisco: Jossey-Bass.

JOYCE, BRUCE, and BEVERLY SHOWERS. 2002. *Student Achievement Through Staff Development.* 3rd ed. Alexandria, VA: Association for Supervision and Curriculum Development.

KORNHABER, M., E. FIERROS, and S. VEENEMA. 2004. *Multiple Intelligences: Best Ideas from Research and Practice.* Needham Heights, MA: Prentice-Hall.

LESSOW-HURLEY, JUDITH. 2003. *Meeting the Needs of Second Language Learners: An Educator's Guide.* Alexandria, VA: Association for Supervision and Curriculum Development.

LEVITT, STEVEN, and STEPHEN DUBNER. 2005. *Freakonomics: A Rogue Economist Explores the Hidden Side of Everything.* New York: HarperCollins.

LYONS, CAROL, and GAY PINNELL. 2001. *Systems for Change in Literacy Education: A Guide to Professional Development.* Portsmouth, NH: Heinemann.

MURPHY, CARLENE, and DALE LICK. 2001. *Whole Faculty Study Groups: Creating Student-Based Professional Development,* 2nd ed. Thousand Oaks, CA: Corwin.

PALMER, PARKER. 1998. *The Courage to Teach.* San Fransisco: Jossey Bass.

PASCHEN, ELISE, and REBEKAH MOSBY. eds. 2001. *Poetry Speaks: Hear Great Poets Read Their Work from Tennyson to Plath.* Naperville: Sourcebooks.

RESTAK, RICHARD. 2003. *The New Brain: How the Modern Age Is Rewiring Your Mind.* New York: Rodale.

RITCHHART, RON. 2002. *Intellectual Character: What It Is, Why It Matters, and How to Get It.* San Francisco: Jossey-Bass.

ROBB, LAURA. 2000. *Redefining Staff Development: A Collaborative Model for Teachers and Administrators.* Portsmouth, NH: Heinemann.

ROSENBLATT, LOUISE. 1938, 1968, 1976. *Literature as Exploration.* New York: Noble and Noble.

SCHON, DONALD. 1987. *Educating the Reflective Practitioner.* San Francisco: Jossey Bass.

SPIELVOGEL, JACKSON. 2005. *World History Journey Across Time: The Early Ages.* Columbus, OH: Glencoe/McGraw-Hill.

TEBBS, TREVOR, and MICHAEL SHAUGHNESSY. 2005. "An Interview with Martha McCarthy: About the High School Survey of Student Engagement." EducationNews.org (June): 1–5.

TOVANI, CHRIS. 2000. *I Read It but I Don't Get It: Comprehension Strategies for Adolescent Readers.* Portland, ME: Stenhouse.

ZULL, JAMES. 2002. *The Art of Changing the Brain: Enriching the Practice of Teaching by Exploring the Biology of Learning.* Sterling, VA: Stylus.

Index